Royal Jousts
at the End of the Fourteenth Century

DEEDS OF ARMS SERIES

Series Editor: Steven Muhlberger, Nipissing University

This series of source readers makes available to a broad audience original accounts of famous displays of martial and chivalric prowess from the Middle Ages and early Renaissance. The books provide short, vivid introductions to particular topics and events, and can also be used in combination to look at the complex phenomenon of chivalric competition. Each volume includes a comprehensive introduction, color gallery of contemporary illustrations, and bibliography for further reading. Five volumes are currently scheduled for publication; others are under consideration.

Check our website for updates: www.freelanceacademypress.com.

DEEDS OF ARMS SERIES   VOLUME 1

Royal Jousts
at the End of the Fourteenth Century

Translated and Edited by Steven Muhlberger

Freelance Academy Press, Inc.
www.FreelanceAcademyPress.com

Cover Illustration: Joust of St. Ingelvert, 1390. Jousting scene. From the *Chronicles* of Jean Froissart. (Bruges, 1470–1475). Location: British Library, London, Great Britain. © HIP / Art Resource, NY

Translations in Chapters 3 and 5 courtesy Will McLean, used with permission.

Freelance Academy Press, Inc., Wheaton, IL 60189
www.freelanceacademypress.com

Printed in the United States of America
by Publishers' Graphics

21 20 19 18 17 16 15 14 13 12   1 2 3 4 5

ISBN 978-1-937439-01-9

Library of Congress Control Number: 2012934208

Contents

List of Illustrations

1.

War, Peace, and Jousting, 1389–90

Royal Jousts brings together some of the most important accounts of medieval jousting.

Considering the importance of formal combat to the medieval aristocracy, we possess surprisingly few detailed accounts of tournaments, jousts or duels. Fans of deeds of arms did enjoy reading or hearing about them, but if our surviving material is any indication, extensive descriptions of the actual events involving contemporary warriors were not what they were looking for. Sometimes, however, there was an upswing of interest that inspired poets and chroniclers to write more detailed descriptions of both combats and accompanying celebrations. These literary treatments are prized, since they give us much of the material that we moderns have used to reconstruct tournaments, jousts, and other deeds of arms over the past two centuries or so.

One particularly rich time for source material are the years 1389–90, when diplomatic competition between Charles VI of France and Richard II of England inspired the kings to sponsor some of the most spectacular formal combats of the entire Middle Ages. These great festivals of arms were elaborately portrayed by a number of writers. As a result, we have valuable descriptions of how jousting was performed and appreciated at the highest social levels in the two great rival kingdoms of the West. These accounts, especially those of the jousts at St. Inglevert, have influenced every modern reconstruction of late medieval jousting.

The literary production of these two years reflects the excitement surrounding Anglo-French relations at a time when it seemed that the Hundred Years War might be ending, thanks to the emergence of two young kings with very different priorities from the leaders of the previous generation. Charles VI of France, whose future insanity was not yet evident, reached his majority in December 1388; Richard II of England threw off the supervision of an unsympathetic group of barons the following May. Neither was enthusiastic about the prospect of further war with the other. There were other projects, perhaps a crusade or an effort to solve the papal schism that divided Europe, which seemed more appealing. It's important to note that few in either court looked forward to a complete end to warfare. Rather, they hoped for a good peace between the rival monarchies, followed by the redirection of martial energy into good and necessary wars, perhaps waged in cooperation with each other against a common foe. The two years in question were marked by successful negotiations for a long truce between England and France, but were also characterized by warlike posturing by both kings, who well knew that they must find some use for the belligerent energies of their nobles. The four great jousts described here, three French and one English, were efforts to rally the warriors of each kingdom behind royal leadership, using the symbolic combats of the joust and attendant lavish celebrations as political propaganda. Sponsorship of these jousts allowed the kings to make peace while striking the kind of proud, warlike pose that their noble subjects expected of them.

These deeds of arms attracted a great deal of attention from contemporary writers and they were not soon forgotten. The reputation of St. Inglevert was lasting enough that some chroniclers of the next generation featured it as one of the most noteworthy events of Charles VI's early reign. The extensive coverage reflects the actual political importance of the jousts. We benefit from this artistic and reportorial effort, which gives us an unprecedented record of festive jousts and the accompanying celebrations. We should not, however, mistake interest and enthusiasm for diligent, accurate reportage. Valuable as these accounts are, they cannot be taken at face value, shaped as they were by the propagandistic intentions of the sponsors and the writers' reliance on a common fund of images and ideas. If, however, we can't quite regard these as dispassionate records, the picture we get still conveys the significance of jousting for both those who took part, and those who witnessed it.

The Joust at St. Denis, May 1389

We should begin by saying that late medieval jousting, like tourneying before it, could be both a celebration of noble identity (which was based on a claimed monopoly on the legitimate waging of war), and at the same time a courtly celebration of love. Where tournaments were mock battles, jousting was in essence a contest between two individuals who were trying to knock each other off their horses. In the early days of the tournament, the twelfth century, there was usually time allocated for "preliminaries," when, before the grand charge that opened the main event, young men eager to gain fame challenged members of the opposing tourney team. It was a good way of attracting attention of one's fellow warriors. In the next century, jousting was so popular that whole meets were devoted to it. The joust became a standard way to celebrate a betrothal or wedding or some other festival. It was also a most suitable place for flirtation and amorous games. By the 1380s, it had long been established that the best warrior deserved the love of beautiful and noble ladies, and that his love in turn was a great prize for his paramour. For kings who wished to mark a new beginning and assert their youthful leadership, jousts which celebrated *armes* and *amour*, the two fields of endeavor in which a young nobleman would naturally seek to excel, were an obvious choice.

The first of King Charles' three great jousts, which took place in May 1389 at the royal monastery of St. Denis, near Paris, combined a celebration of the French dynasty's military tradition, a commitment to further martial accomplishment, and a flashy gala on the theme of *amour*. Past and future wars were celebrated by the combination of a solemn funeral for the late Charles V's great general, Bertrand du Guesclin, with a grand knighting of the current king's cousin Louis of Anjou, who was claiming the Kingdom of Sicily. The combination of funeral and knighting was hardly coincidental; Bertrand had died nine years earlier and despite the show of royal support, Louis was not about to receive any substantial aid for his Italian ambitions. The St. Denis event was about King Charles and the chivalric and amorous court that surrounded him; it was an advertisement of the glory of France under a young and virile king.

The two documents associated with this occasion that are included here make much of the combination of *armes* and *amour* at St. Denis. The first is a poetic invitation to the joust by the prominent court poet Eustache Deschamps. The joust in Deschamps' presentation is to be a "sweet new thing," a fresh beginning under a new king. The clear theme evoked in the poem is the erotic connection between martial prowess and the love of fair ladies.

And this was no false advertising, as we see in the second document, an excerpt from the Chronicle of St. Denis, the very monastery where the joust took place. The monastery was a royal institution, and its chronicle, composed by a series of anonymous monks, had a semi-official character. The chronicler of the moment quite naturally had an obligation to record the magnificence of the occasion. He used his most ornate Latin to praise the vigor of the male participants, the beauty of the ladies who accompanied them, the gorgeous and color-coordinated costumes, and the formal parade that opened the first of three days of jousting. Yet the Monk of St. Denis found something distasteful and vaguely pagan about the whole affair, especially since the whole event ended on the last night with an outburst of licentiousness. Of course the Monk had to disapprove of "abominable adultery" within his own monastery; but as his own account makes clear, the king was very pleased. A grand joust decorated by beautiful ladies and ending in a memorable party was an appropriate inspiration and reward for the heroes of a new age.

The Joust Accompanying Queen Isabella's Entry into Paris, August 1389

A few months later, King Charles sponsored another joust in Paris in conjunction with a politically important celebration, the formal entry of his queen, Isabella of Bavaria, into the capital city. This occasion, like other entries of the later Middle Ages, was not actually the occasion of Isabella's first visit to Paris, or even her first visit as queen. It was rather a celebration of the dynasty, of a great city, and of their special relationship—the latter being something that needed cultivating, since Paris' good will toward its rulers could never be taken for granted. At the same time, hopes for peace with England were high, because the prominent warrior and diplomat Jean de Châteaumorand was finishing negotiations for a long-term truce.

The entry is recorded by Jean Froissart, who wrote one of his most elaborate passages as an attempt to convey the scale and sensuousness of the parade, the gifts given, and the feasts. He is our source for the military pageants that took place. These included a reenactment of a battle with King Saladin, and a play of the Trojan War in the feasting hall, in which a ship containing one hundred men at arms attacked a castle which was "gallantly defended."

We cannot be sure whether the pageants had any element of real competition, but the entry also included three days of jousting. As in the case of the joust at St. Denis, we have a poem by Deschamps that probably is an invitation to potential participants in the combats. (Note, however, that what Deschamps said was planned differs from what Froissart reports actually took place.) The poem, like the invitation to the St. Denis joust, evokes the presence of fine and beautiful ladies but rather than hint at erotic possibilities, Deschamps speaks of "a queen dressed like an angel" who with an entourage of thirty others will preside over the festivities. The poem also envisions that a "noble knight of the Eagle of Gold," no doubt the king himself, would lead chosen knights and squires all in the same livery to defend the field against all challengers. Some details of the competition are given, including the fact that foreign knights were specifically invited. Unlike the St. Denis joust, the competitions at Paris were explicitly being presented to all of Europe.

Europe was no doubt impressed; yet these jousts were not enough to satisfy the French court.

The Joust at St. Inglevert, March–April 1390

The third French-sponsored series of jousts of the period we are discussing, the jousts at St. Inglevert, were the most elaborate and are the most famous. For this, Jean Froissart gets much of the credit—or bears much of the responsibility. His account is huge, and unlike almost any other surviving description of jousting, tells his audience blow-by-blow what happened in the lists—who struck who, who raised sparks from his opponent's helm, who broke his lance and how well, and so forth. If it is difficult for modern readers to absorb and visualize all these details, Froissart's recounting of the deeds at St. Inglevert gives a convincing picture of what it must really have been like when famous champions met in the lists. St. Inglevert, by default of alternatives, stands in for every unrecorded jousting match of the later Middle Ages.

Saint-Inglevert was indeed an extraordinarily prominent event, and came by its prominence honestly, because it electrified chivalrically-minded writers both of the time and also of the next generation. Financed and promoted energetically by King Charles, and involving important members of his entourage, the joust attracted the attention of much of aristocratic Europe as soon as it was announced. Likewise the joust's organizer was careful to publicize the results, so that those who had not attended would have their curiosity satisfied, and be duly impressed. The action was recorded by two heralds, and their record of courses run and strokes landed on shields or helms seems to have been widely available, serving Froissart among others as source material for more finished accounts. And there were several finished accounts. In the immediate aftermath, not only Froissart but two other chroniclers, the Monk of St. Denis and an anonymous poet, put out their own versions of the story. In later years, when the political climate had change drastically, three other writers still found St. Inglevert a good subject for the exercise of their eloquence. These were the anonymous authors of the *Chronographia Regum Francorum* (after 1399) and the *Book of the Deeds of Boucicaut* (1409), and Jean Juvénal des Ursins, a prominent bishop and politician who wrote a *History of Charles VI* about 1422. St. Inglevert is not only the subject of the longest description of any joust, we are able to see it from multiple points of view.

One consequence of this is to undermine our naïve faith in Froissart's account. There are enough differences between what he says and what others do to show us that the famous chronicler altered at least some of the facts to suit his ideas of what a first-class joust should be like. For instance, Froissart says that the joust took place in May, the beautiful month; it actually took place in March and April, a fairly normal time for such events. Both Froissart and the Monk of St. Denis show that one knight (and one knight only) on the visitors' side was severely criticized for breaking rules. However, Froissart and the Monk tell entirely different stories about the trespass and each identifies a different knight as the offender. Froissart and the other five chroniclers seem to have altered the facts about St. Inglevert to suit their ideas of what a perfect joust should be; or perhaps, what a perfect jousting story should be like.

The facts are pretty impressive as they are. Three chamberlains, young knights in the service of King Charles, took upon themselves to challenge all foreign knights to come and meet them over the course of a month. The three were Boucicaut (Jean le Maingre the younger), Renaud de Roye, and the lord de Sempy, among the most daring and belligerent French warriors of the time, men who had shown themselves in the 1380s as willing to go anywhere for a fight, in hopes of winning renown and advancement. Some of the writers present the challenge as a product of their individual courage and ambition. There is reason to think, however, that they were reacting to the fact that English visitors to France during this time of truce often bragged about English success at arms and the inability or unwillingness of Frenchmen to meet them. What became a challenge to the entire chivalric world may well have begun as a challenge aimed directly at the English; and indeed the actual event was sited near English-held

Calais and seems to have attracted only Englishmen and their allies. Although the king and his more sober advisers did their best to recast the challenge so as to defuse any outbreak of real hostility, issues of national pride lurked in the background, with the possibility that the fragile truce or the long hoped-for permanent peace might be threatened by the rivalry of a formal deed of arms.

Once the challenge was established as one of three Frenchmen against the whole world, and not as a dangerous one aimed solely at the traditional enemy, King Charles was enthusiastic to support it, to the substantial sum of ten thousand francs. It was precisely the kind of grandiose enterprise that would appeal to a king who Froissart himself called "young and giddy." At the same time, we should reflect on how hosting such an event—even at one remove—could increase a royal reputation for generosity. And in fact, Froissart maintains that many English warriors accepted the challenge in a very positive spirit: "Let us prepare ourselves to go to this place near Calais," he has some of them say, "for these French knights only hold [this joust] that they may have our company: it is well done, and shows that they are good companions. Let us not disappoint them!"

The turnout in fact was incredible. Froissart refers to one hundred and more English knights and squires who were interested in participating. That vague number seems to be closer to reality than Froissart's total of thirty-nine named jousters. An anonymous poet says 105 took part, but he only lists one hundred. However, his list is very close to one of 102 names provided by the Monk of St. Denis. The three challengers and their backers were ready and able to manage this outpouring of chivalric enthusiasm. One of the features of the St. Inglevert joust that has always attracted much attention was the use of heralds and heraldic symbolism to organize the activities. Separate shields which symbolized jousts of peace (that is, with blunted lances or *rochets*) and jousts of war (with sharp lances) were set out, and each foreign visitor struck the shield corresponding to the type of the combat they wished to engage in. Two different procedures are detailed, by Froissart on one hand and the Monk, the writer of the *Chronographia Regum Francorum*, and the anonymous poet

on the other. Whichever is closer to the truth, the organizers were clearly interested in producing a dramatic and ceremonious effect. It is unlikely that this
kind of preparation was unprecedented for deeds of arms, but certainly the St.
Inglevert event seems to have served as a model for later events. In the fifteenth
century, we see a number of fashionable *pas d'armes* (dramatized challenges
where warriors, usually on foot, defended a narrow place) lovingly designed
and equally lovingly described.

If the three jousters and the king behind them were hoping for an event that
would gain the attention of Europe, they got one. Some of this is due to both the
setting and the generous hospitality, which was arranged, according to the poet,
by notable *maîtres d' hôtel*. Far more important, however, was the astonishing
athletic performance of the Frenchmen. In a single month, they jousted for at
least eleven and perhaps thirteen days, running in the vicinity of five hundred
courses, all of them with steel lances, since no one seems to have taken the
easier option. Froissart's incomplete and probably fictionalized description of
three days' jousting names eighteen foreign riders who were knocked out of
their saddles; no one tells us that any of the three Frenchmen were unhorsed
at any time. Two accounts tell us that the French sailed through the month
without injury; two others disagree. Froissart describes a few injuries suffered
on either side, including one that forced Renaud de Roye to take a break. One
gets the impression from Froissart that the injuries were not very significant.
The Monk of St. Denis, taking perhaps a different rhetorical tack, praises the
French champions by emphasizing the sufferings Boucicaut and Roye had to
overcome. The Monk states that these two were bedridden for nine days following injuries received on the fifth day of jousting, leaving the lord de Sempy
to take up the slack until his companions returned.

The immediate result of this great assembly of arms was entirely positive.
Those, like the Monk of St. Denis, who feared that the challenge was beyond
the strength of the champions, whose defeat would prove them presumptuous,
did not see their fears realized. Nor did the competition, as the "most prudent"
members the king's council had feared, end up exacerbating hostilities with

England or derailing ongoing negotiations for a permanent peace treaty. The goodwill depicted by Froissart, based on mutual appreciation of skill at arms, even in a former enemy, seems to have been real. When, a month after the jousts, the duke of Bourbon led a crusading expedition to Tunisia, there were in his army a number of English lords who had heard of the plan when they had recently been at Calais. The meeting that had just taken place at St. Inglevert had clearly not hurt the cause of Anglo-French peace. If relations between the two kingdoms soured soon after, the three French champions cannot be blamed.

Beyond the politics of the moment, St. Inglevert and the literary accounts thereof can be seen as a validation and reemphasis of the place of individual martial competition and reputation in the culture of the time. Quite interesting is the curious opening passage of the anonymous verse account of the joust. The poet begins by claiming that he met some shepherds and shepherdesses on the way to St. Inglevert, who lived untouched by the troubles of the world. They had heard the news of St. Inglevert, an unprecedented and dangerous deed of arms, and were impressed. The shepherdesses were now dissatisfied with their peaceful activities and with their beaus, who had not earned love by martial accomplishment. Once again we see the connection between virility and participation in formal combats. Even carefree shepherds and shepherdesses pay tribute to Boucicaut, Roye, and Sempy, who at St. Inglevert have created an ideal world centered on the joust.

The Joust at Smithfield near London, October 1390

The jousts of 1389–90 were manifestations of French royal power and undoubtedly provoked envy as well as admiration. Richard II, despite the fact that he was willing collaborator with Charles VI in an effort to end the war between the two dynasties, could hardly leave such French exhibitionism unanswered. Richard in fact took a number of practical initiatives to limit French influence in the Low Countries and in Italy. On the symbolic level, too, Charles had to be answered. Thus in 1390, Richard and the royal council decided to advertise a great international joust to be held at Smithfield just outside of London, the structure of which shows that the English court had been paying close attention to the French celebrations, and felt the need to match them with an event on a similar scale.

In planning this joust, Richard was playing to both foreign and domestic audiences. English chroniclers emphasize Richard's efforts to attract and dispense noteworthy hospitality to "all manner of foreigners." Froissart, who wrote the most extensive description of the event, also paid much attention to French participation, and devoted pages to the foreign policy consequences of the celebration; namely, how the French took offense when the count d'Ostrevant—ruler of Froissart's native Hainault and normally a close ally of the duke of Burgundy—was especially honored by Richard by being inducted into the Order of the Garter. Froissart is insistent that the young count meant no harm by accepting such honors from King Richard, but he also shows that the count had been warned that even taking part in Richard's joust might get him into trouble with his French friends. The whole incident is an excellent example of how ostensibly friendly formal combats were taken very seriously by the movers and shakers of the day. Given the reaction of the French, one can hardly doubt that Richard's joust was seen by all concerned as, in part, a diplomatic initiative.

At the same time, the Smithfield joust had a message for its English audience. Richard, who famously was criticized for not taking a much more aggressive stance towards France, used the joust to demonstrate that he was the master of English chivalry. Archival records and chronicles indicate that in the year of St. Inglevert, some of Richard's highest-ranking nobles had been demonstrating their bellicosity and their worth by seeking out challenges with prominent foreigners, particularly Scots. The Westminster Chronicle shows the king, whose license was necessary for such competitions to take place, trying to put an end to these dangerous games, which might have incalculable consequences. The king's desire to control an all-too-independent military aristocracy was part of the motive for the Smithfield joust. Chivalric pride and energy could not be discouraged, but it could be redirected through traditional means to serve royal purposes.

Richard's domestic strategy is evident in the way he reused ceremonial elements from his rival's festivities at St. Denis and Paris. As at St. Denis, ladies led tethered knights into the lists, all of them wearing livery marked with a royal badge. As in Deschamps' poetic announcement of the Parisian entry, the chief figure at Smithfield was advertised as an anonymous knight, who was obviously the king. Richard was clearly influenced by the design of the French celebrations, but he used the elements he took from them for a very specific English purpose: the twenty most prominent English defenders of the lists against foreign challengers, who were also the participants in the ceremonial procession, were all members of the Order of the Garter, the senior active chivalric order of Europe and a link to the consecrated past of Richard's dynasty. In his mustering of the Order, as well as in the use of royal heraldry by all the leading English champions, Richard was claiming, as well he might, ownership of the proud English military tradition of his father's and grandfather's time. Richard II thus deftly used the formal language of arms to communicate a favorable image to with potential foreign allies and his own sometimes unruly subjects. This alone may call for a reexamination of the common idea that he was less chivalrously inclined than other English princes of the late fourteenth century.

In this case as in previous ones, we find that formal combats were taken extremely seriously: they were war, diplomacy, or domestic politics in a different form. If we think about it, this situation is perhaps less exotic than it may seem at first glance. Few people are dispassionate about Olympic medal standings when it is a matter of national pride. Many politicians are keen to produce winning teams and thereby enjoy some reflected glory. Even the location and richness of the games is a matter of intense interest, among the leadership and general public. Perhaps the most significant difference between festive jousts and more recent forms of politicized sport is that in the fourteenth century, the rulers were very often competitors, and that the line between the competition and actual warfare was sometimes very unclear.

Some Notes on the Translations

I am responsible for the translations appearing here, but I should be clear where I benefited from the work of others. Will McLean kindly gave permission for me to use his translations of Deschamps' invitation to the St. Denis joust and the cry for the Smithfield joust. The translation of Deschamps' poem advertising the entry into Paris comes from W.C. Meller, *A Knight's Life in the Days of Chivalry* (New York, 1924) 128–9.

My translation of Froissart's *Chronicles* is an adaptation of Thomas Johnes's of 1805. There are many differences between my version and Johnes's, but I began my work on Froissart with his nineteenth-century fan, and it would be absurd and ungrateful not to acknowledge that I have often leaned on him.

In regard to proper names, unless I have been quite sure what the usual, modern forms of names are, I have left them as I found them in the editions. Better scholars than I have tried to track down the identities of the participants at St. Inglevert, without a lot of success. As the anonymous poet indicates, French writers had great difficulty when faced with English names. Could Froissart, I wonder, really tell the difference between the names Clifton, Clifford, and Clinton? (And who can blame him if he couldn't?) I have called Englishmen "John" and Frenchmen "Jean" even if it is probably an anachronistic distinction.

One unfamiliar usage, the terms "within" and "without," should be explained. Jousts were structured as competitions between two sides, which were usually called "those within," (*dedans*) referring to the tenants or the home team, and "those without," (*dehors*) who were the opponents or the visitors.

2.◆
The Joust at St. Denis, May 1389

Deschamps' Poetic Invitation

Arms, amours, joy and pleasure,

Hope, desire, remembrance, hardiness,

Youth also, manners and bearing

Humble glances cast lovingly

Fine persons and fair, adorned richly

Bethink ye of this new-come season

This Mayday, this great and beautiful feast,

Which by the king is held at St. Denis,

Joust well and maintain your cause,

Thus will ye be honored and held dear.

For there will be the great beauty of France,

Knights are coming and ladies also

Who will present themselves armed as is ordained

At the proper place all in gala array

The first day; and on the second

Come the squires with each his demoiselle

In tournament array and the joy is renewed,

And there will the heralds utter many shouts

To those who joust well, "keep firm in your saddles

And ye will be honored and held dear."

Now there may be those who wield well the lance

And who maneuver skillfully

To gain Love's favor

And who will bear harness a long time

These shall have praise and fair looks;

Rightly shall such be shown them;

Love who wavers not shall enflame them with amorous aspirations,

Honor shall be given them, to those who do best, the prizes,

Take heed, all, of this sweet new thing

And ye shall be honored and held dear.

ENVOY

Servants of love! look longingly

On the angelic Beauties of Paradise.

Then joust manfully and joyously

And ye shall be honored and held dear.

The Monk of St. Denis' Account of the St. Denis Joust

On Monday, around the ninth hour, just as had been announced, the king ordered the performance of *hastiludes* ["spear games," in this case, "jousts" –ed.] by twenty-two knights of proven vigor, who since they were skilled and able with such gear would make the occasion glorious. And they hastened to carry through this project.

Riding plumed horses and wearing golden gleaming armor and green shields blazoned with the badge of the king, and followed by squires who ceremoniously carried their lances and helms, the knights approached the king in the first court of the abbey, and since they had lately strayed far afield in the wantonness of dissolute conduct, as men did in ancient times, they thought it good to dally for some time with the brilliant throng of ladies who were there to lead them into the lists. These ladies by royal order were of the same number as the knights, and dressed similarly in very dark green, with festoons of gold and gems, and mounted on horses adorned in the appointed royal manner, were led into the king's presence. And if you had seen their beauty and simplicity of bearing, you would have said that the false concubinage and rites of the goddesses of long ago had beyond doubt been restored.

Of the knights named by the king, those of the first rank were the dukes of Touraine and Bourbon [and several others]. With them were these ladies especially distinguished by the nobility of their families ... As they had been instructed, they took silk cords from their breasts and sweetly gave them to the aforesaid knights, and rode on their left until they had come to the lists. Following the first group of lords [was another] ... Noble ladies ... led these knights to the lists accompanied by a retinue of many musicians with trumpets and other musical instruments, playing melodies of inestimable charm.

Then warlike ardor urged on the spirits of the charging knights, and they bought the renown of praise and worth with repeated thrusts of their lances, even to the extent of being knocked to the ground. After dinner, the ladies and damsels, on whose judgement the choosing of champions depended, named from the foreigners and natives two knights whom they thought should be particularly honored and prized. The king heard the decision with pleasure, and desired to add to it with his accustomed generosity. He endowed the aforesaid illustrious men with great gifts in accordance with their merits. And then after dinner, the rest of the night was spent in dancing and performances.

Following the first set of jousts, the second day was devoted to similar combats between twenty-two chosen squires. Because they had devoted themselves so closely to the service of the knights who fought the previous day, the squires assumed their armor and horses and with the same ceremony were led to the field by an equal number of damsels. The squires jousted with each other until nightfall. There was a sumptuous dinner in royal style, during which the ladies named those who should be prized over the others. And because the king had ordered three days of jousting, on the following day the previous arrangement was not observed, but knights and squires took part together in the games, and as before, those whom the ladies thought had carried themselves more valiantly received prizes for valor.

The fourth night ended with dances and licentious exploits, which in fact should more appropriately be recited by the bellowing of tragedians than included in the truthful record of the historian. Many prudent men, however, have agreed that in this case those exploits should not be passed by in silence, but that they should be presented as an example for people of the future to follow or avoid, though I counsel the latter. Thus I will tell the truth of these deeds. When they had changed night into day, and mixed too much drink with the banqueting, Father Bacchus gave rise to so much intemperance that many shamelessly and indiscriminately polluted the royal abbey and indulged in illicit sex and abominable adultery.

Nevertheless, in order that this licentious occasion should be remembered long and affectionately, the king, at lunch on the following day, praised the knights and squires, each in according to his merit, and presented many gifts. And with a liberal hand and royal generosity he gave the ladies and damsels bracelets and tokens of gold and silver, and silken material. He said farewell and gave kisses of peace to the more illustrious, and gave them leave to visit again.

3.

The Joust Accompanying Queen Isabella's Entry into Paris, August 1389

Deschamps' Poetic Invitation

Translation by Will McLean

PROCLAMATION OF A TOURNEY AT PARIS

Let every foreign knight and squire
And everyone that seeks renown
Hark, hark to the honor and the praise
Of the great festival of arms
It is decreed by the noble knight
Of the Eagle of Gold, that his company

On thirty destriers ready to joust
And dressed alike in one livery
Shall deliver all of their own profession
Just after the day of Magdalene.

In the noble city, that as you know
Bears Paris as its proper name
There shall be a queen dressed like an angel
And thirty ladies in like array.
The Secret Isle will be revealed,
You'll learn its name. On Sunday dance,
On Monday joust for noble gifts
As many lances as you desire
Just after the day of Magdalene.

Who jousts best from without, without exchange
shall win a chaplet of fine good gold
From within, a diamond lozenge-set
From the hand of the queen to have and hold.
And those that come from foreign lands
Fifteen days to come and as many away
Safe conduct shall have, with no treachery
So the Eagle of Gold shall proclaim
Just after the day of Magdalene.

On the following day the squires will come
For Tuesday's joust will be arranged
A squire, and thirty more in ranks
Clothed alike in one livery
Shall dress themselves full readily.
A damsel of body lightsome and fine
And thirty more dressed like she

Will consider and view the noble jousts
Just after the day of Magdalene.

The best jouster without will not win wool
But a chaplet of silver as diadem
Within: a clasp of purest gold
The damsel will give it, so they say.
The Eagle of Gold will give a feast
On Monday night if you wish to stay
The king of France will hold his court.
On Tuesday night, it is proclaimed
Just after the day of Magdalene.

ENVOY

Princes who wish to do great deeds
We counsel you: attend that day.
Knights, a warrior will understand
The time for big things is not far away.
Hear our advice. Mark what we say.
Just after the day of Magdalene.

Froissart's Account of the Jousts at Paris

I will name the knights of who were "within" and defending, who were styled the Knights of the Golden Sun. And although this was at that time the heraldic device of the king, he was "without" and jousted with the challengers just now, to gain renown through arms, and have an adventure. These were the thirty knights ...

All the knights were armed, and their shields were adorned with a splendid sun. At three o'clock, they entered the square of St. Catherine, where the queen had already arrived in a magnificent car, and the duchesses and other ladies in great state, and taken their places on the seats prepared for them. The king of

France next made his appearance completely equipped for jousting, of which amusement he was very fond.

The jousts now began, and were carried on with vigour, for there were many knights from foreign parts. Sir Jean de Hainault, count d'Ostrevant, jousted right well, as did those knights who had accompanied him, such as the lord de Gommines, Sir Jean d'Andregines, the lord de Cantan, Sir Ansol de Trans-segines, and Sir Clinquart de Herinno. Every one performed his part, in honor of the ladies; and the duke of Ireland jousted well: he was then residing in France with the king, and had been summoned to be present. A German knight from beyond the Rhine, called Sir Servais de Mirande, gained great commendation. The jousts were strong and unyielding and well-ridden, but there were so many knights that it was difficult to give a full stroke, and the dust was so trouble-some that it increased their difficulties. The lord de Coucy shone with brilliancy. The jousts were continued without relaxation until night, when the ladies were conducted to their hôtels.

The queen of France and her attendants were led back to the hôtel of St. Pol, where was the most magnificent banquet for the ladies ever heard of. The feast and dancing lasted until sunrise, and the prize for the jousting was given, with the assent of the ladies and heralds, to the king, as being the best jouster "without," and the prize for those "within" was given to the Haze of Flanders, bastard-brother to the duchess of Burgundy.

On account of the complaints the knights made of the dust which had pre-vented many from exerting themselves that day, the king ordered the lists to be watered. Two hundred water-carriers were employed on the Wednesday to water the square, but, notwithstanding their efforts, there was still plenty of dust.

The count de St. Pol arrived this Wednesday straight from England, having made haste to be present at these festivities, and had left Sir Jean de Château-morand to follow with the treaty of the truce. The count de St. Pol was kindly received by the king and his lords: his countess, who had been near the person of the queen at these festivals, was the best pleased at his arrival. In the afternoon of the Wednesday, thirty squires, who had been in attendance the preceding day, advanced to the lists where the tournaments had been held, whither the ladies also came, in the same state, and seated themselves as before. The jousting was ably and vigorously kept up until night, when the company returned to hôtels. The banquet for the ladies this evening at the hôtel de St. Pol was as grand as the preceding one, and the prize for those "without" was adjudged by the ladies and heralds to a squire from Hainault, who had accompanied the count d'Ostrevant, called Jean de Floyon, and for those within, to a squire belonging to the duke of Burgundy, called Jean de Poulceres.

Then, on Thursday, knights and squires jousted promiscuously, and many gallant jousts were done, for every one took pains to excel. Night put an end to it, and there was a grand banquet again for the ladies, at the hôtel de St. Pol, when the prize for those "without" was given to Sir Charles des Armoyes, and for those "within" to an esquire of the queen of France, named Kouk.

On the Friday, the king feasted the ladies and damsels at dinner, which was very splendid and plentiful. Towards the end of it, as the king was seated at table, with the duchess of Berry, the duchess of Burgundy, the duchess of Touraine, the countess de Saint Pol, the lady of Coucy, and many more, two mounted knights, completely armed for the joust and with lances in their hands, entered the hall, (which was very spacious, having been, as I have said, erected for the occasion). One was Sir Renaud de Roye, the other Sir Boucicaut the younger. Having jousted bravely for some time, they were joined by Sir Renaud de Trye, Sir William de Namur, Sir Charles des Armoyes, the lord de Garencieres, the lord de Nantonillet, Sir Jean de Barbenton, and several others, who gallantly jousted for two hours before the king and ladies; and, when they had sufficiently amused themselves, they returned to their hôtels.

The ladies and damsels took their leave, this Friday, of the king and queen, as did such lords as pleased, and returned to their homes. The king and queen thanked very graciously such as took their leave, for having come to this celebration and conversing with them.

4.
◆

The Joust at St. Inglevert, March–April 1390

Froissart on the Preparations for the Joust

The king of France resided at Montpellier upwards of twelve days ... He and his people too were pleased by the way of life of the city, the ladies and damsels, and the amusements that they found there. The king, who still had a lot to learn, was at this time young and giddy. So he danced and caroled with these frisky ladies of Montpellier all night. He entertained them with handsome suppers and banquets, and presented to those most in his favor rings and clasps of gold. He acquired so greatly the love of the Montpellier ladies that some wished he had made a longer stay, for there were revels, dances, carols, and entertainments every day and night the whole time he was there.

You know, or must have heard it mentioned many times, that association with ladies and damsels encourages the hearts of young gentlemen, and raises them up to desire and seek out all honor. I say this because the king had in his company three young gentlemen of good character, high enterprise, and great valor, and they show this well, as I shall relate.

The names of these three knights were Sir Boucicaut the younger, Sir Renaud de Roye, and the lord de Sempy. These knights were chamberlains to the king, who loved and valued them highly for they very well prepared him and served him in arms and in all other ways that knights should serve their lord. While they were at Montpellier amusing themselves with the ladies and damsels, they were aroused to take arms in the course of the ensuing summer: the principal cause of this, as I was informed, was as follows. [Froissart never precisely defines the "principal cause," but tells a very long story about how several years earlier, an English knight, Peter Courtenay, who bragged that no French knight had ever been willing to meet him, met his comeuppance at the hands of the French lord de Clary, who fought a secret joust against Courtenay. Both the Monk of St. Denis (below) and the later historian Jean Juvénal des Ursins (not included) indicate that in 1390 Englishmen were still disparaging the courage of the French chivalry. –ed.]

During the stay of the king of France at Montpellier, he gave a grand banquet to many ladies and damsels of that town; during which, all I have just related was talked over, and with the following result.

Sir Boucicaut the younger, Sir Renaud de Roye, and the lord de Sempy, offered to hold a field of arms on the frontier of Calais, in the course of the ensuing summer, against all foreign knights and squires, for the space of thirty days, and to joust with lances of peace or war. The king of France, as well as those present, thinking this proposal was rather presumptuous, remonstrated with them, and desired they would put down their challenge on paper, that if any improper language were made use of, it might be corrected; for the king and his council wished to examine it, being unwilling that any improper or unusual terms should be used. The three knights agreed that this would be right, and, in reply to the king, said they would instantly obey his commands. They ordered a clerk, with pens, paper, and ink, into another apartment, and dictated to him as follows:

From the great desire we have to become acquainted with the nobles, gentlemen, knights, and squires of the kingdom of France, as well as with those of other realms far and near, we propose being at St. Inglevert the twentieth day of May next ensuing, and to remain there for thirty days complete; and on each of these thirty days, excepting the Fridays, we will deliver from their vows all foreign knights, squires, and gentlemen, from whatever countries they may come, with five courses with a sharp or blunt lance, whichever pleases them better, or with both lances if more agreeable.

On the outside of our accommodations will be hung our shields, blazoned with our arms; that is to say, with our targets of war and our shields of peace. Whoever may choose to joust with us has only to come, or send any one, the preceding day, to touch with a rod either of these shields, as he wishes. If he touches the target of war, he shall find an opponent ready on the morrow to engage him in a joust of war: and if he touches the shield of peace, he shall be jousted with a blunted lance; and if both shields are touched, he shall be accommodated with both sorts of combat. Every one who may come, or send to touch our shields, must give his name to the persons who shall be appointed to look after the shields. And all such foreign knights and squires as shall be desirous of jousting with us shall bring with them some noble friend, and we will do the same on our parts, who regulate the entire affair.

We particularly entreat such noble knights or squires as may accept our challenge, to believe that we do not make it through presumption, pride, or any ill will, but solely with a view of having their honorable company, and making acquaintance with them, which we desire from the bottom of our hearts. None of our targets shall be covered with steel or iron, any more than those who may joust with us; nor shall there be any fraud, deceit, or trick made use of, as judged by those who have been commissioned to supervise and judge. And that all gentlemen, knights, and squires, to whom these presents shall come, may depend on their authenticity, we have set to them our seals, with our arms, this twentieth day of November, at Montpellier, in the year of grace 1389.

Underneath was signed, Renaud de Roye, Boucicaut, Sempy.

The king of France was well pleased with this courageous enterprise of his three knights, though before he was willing to concede that the affair should go any further the matter was looked over, examined and scrutinized so that no fault could be found in the terms. It was objected to by some of the council, that it was not reasonable that the deed of arms should be performed so close to Calais, and that the English might take this as hostility arising from arrogance and presumption, and that this should be taken into consideration, for a truce of three years had been agreed between France and England. This matter should be scrutinized, lest anything be done that might stir up dissension between the two realms. The king's ministers were one whole day considering the matter, without coming to any conclusion. Some of the most prudent said that it was not good to go along with all the projects of young knights, for more evil than good might ensue from them … The king, however, who was young himself, was favourably inclined towards them, and said, "Let them perform their enterprise: they are young and courageous, and, besides, have vowed it before the ladies of Montpellier. We are desirous that this thing should go forward and be carried out as best as they are able."

When the king had thus declared his mind to the council, no one made further opposition, to the great joy of the knights. The challenge having been agreed to in the manner the knights had drawn it out, the king called them into his closet, and said, "Boucicaut, Renaud, and Sempy, be attentive in this your enterprise, to guard well your own honor and that of our kingdom: let nothing be spared in the state you keep; for I will not fail to assist you as far as ten thousand francs." The three knights cast themselves on their knees and returned the king their warmest thanks.

Chronographia Regum Francorum on St. Inglevert

In that same year, 1390, three knights of King Charles of France, his chamberlains, namely Boucicaut the greater, who not long afterward was appointed marshal of France, Renaud de Roye, and the lord de Sempy manfully performed a deed worthy of recitation. For they performed this deed against all foreigners, from England, Denmark, Germany, Bohemia, Poland and all regions and countries of Christendom who gathered at the end of February at St. Inglevert, a religious house located between Boulogne on the sea and Calais. These people came from everywhere having news of the upcoming deed through herald of the duke of Lancaster, who was called in French "Lincastre," namely that the three were prepared to meet everyone of whatever condition, as long as they were nobles, who would come to them over a thirty day period, beginning on the first of March, and excepting Sundays and holy days, and who wished to perform courses with sharp lances or others with blunt ones. And the following conditions were set forth: that if any of the three of them for whatever cause should be rendered unable to joust during the thirty days of the festival, the other two would be obligated to fulfill the courses of the rest of the comers, however many there were; and that if two of them were incapable the third nevertheless would have all those courses of the lances aforesaid for withstanding the comers and fulfilling their courses. And it was added that he who ran out of bounds, either within or without, should lose his horse; and if anyone killed the horse of his opponent, he should give full compensation, either out of his own funds or from that of the comers as a group.

And so that these three should have firm notice, however late, of what they were committed to do on the morrow, there was in an open area well-suited for jousting a certain spruce tree, which was beautiful, branchy and well-shaped, in which it was arranged that two shields should hang, one for blunt lances for the joust of peace, and the other for sharp steel for the joust of war; and any noble coming to this spruce tree should touch which of the two shields he wished with a certain wand which he would find ready there, and a certain herald was placed among the branches at the highest point of the spruce tree waiting from sunrise to sunset and he should respond to anyone touching the shields by asking who he was and from what country, and that one should tell the herald his name, country, and family, and whether he was noble by name or by arms. And the herald should immediately write this down in his papers and always late in the day report to his three masters who were named above.

Indeed a very large number of noble knights and squires from different regions outside of the kingdom of France came together in that place to take part in this jousting and to test the prowess of these men at arms; and especially the English came. Among them, just like the rest, came the earl of Derby, the heir of the aforesaid duke of Lancaster, who was soon to be king of England, as will be reported below. He gave the Frenchmen from his largesse many great gifts.

But these three knights, failing in nothing, so mightily and valorously conducted themselves in this deed, in which they overcame all the others who came, both by their vigor in arms and by their lavish banquets and gifts, through the generosity of the aforesaid king, that they were commended with praises from abroad and heaped up the highest possible honor and glory for his consecrated Gallic realm.

An Anonymous Poem on St. Inglevert

Near Ardres, in a field
Ten days before the month of April
In the year 1390
I saw that many shepherds
Found great frolics
Dancing and singing nobly
And held pleasant pastorelle.
The most beautiful shepherdess
There asked me

"Do you come to see the series
Of jousts? For a long time
There has not been such a joust
With lance of steel."

I answered: "Nay, my dear,
But I ask you please
For the sake of love,
Tell me the truth about it
By your courtesy.
What do people say of it?"
Then she told me:
"Believe it,
The Frenchmen have the honor
Until now, for a long time
There was not so cruel an enterprise,
Nor one so mortal.
I do not remember that there ever was,
Since I was a maid,
Such a joust with lance of steel."

Then a jolly shepherdess
Said to her beau
"Don't you boast of my love without contradiction
When you don't perform any charges for me.
I repent of my love for you
When you wait so long
To go jousting in a high saddle
At this ceremonious joust.
Now there ought to be no doubt that
For love of a maiden
one should joust with lance of steel.

"This shepherd with whom she was not pleased

Answered: "It is a perilous trick [408]

To joust up there, by St. Hellie.

Yesterday eve Andrew le Sours said

He never saw such courage

As at this joust, for yesterday

He was present at the field of battle

And Lady Anchelle, his wife,

Told me the news. Lady, believe it,

That never was in the realm of France more fierce

Jousting done with lance of steel.

"What's the point my dear, I ask you

Of the running of such a joust?

I am prolonging my life

I give it up, for indeed fear

Of death forbids me to joust.

These three retainers

Of the noble king of France

If they achieve their goal,

They ought to have

All love perpetual, without inconstancy

When they against the English,

Have so well jousted with lance of steel."

In the past people have spoken of

And still often make much

Of courage and of enterprises

Of many who have reigned very valiantly.

But now one is able to speak well

Of valour, concerning this affair,

For the undertaking

Is strongly to be praised.

For a long time, nothing was taken to such an end

Nowhere was anything so strongly sought out,

Nothing lasted so long

As that which I wish to speak.

The place was called St. Inglevert

In which three knights of France

Whom one ought to praise highly

And who were worthy of commendation

Awaited thirty full days all foreigners

Who against them, on charging destriers,

Wished to come there to joust

Five full courses with steel lances.

For each man willingly

They have accepted without turning away;

And so there were by great courtesy,

Many lords of grand lineage

Come straight from England

Hoping, I assure you, to go

From there immediately

Having vanquished our chivalry,

But well they have been

Received with steel lance

And with the shield so vigorously

And without a doubt by strength and virtue,

So that the truth of it was learned well,

Even by the strongest of their party.

And such friendship appeared in the field

That two shields also hung from one pine.

The one represented the lance of steel,

The other shield was marked

For the rochets of friendship.

But no one who was there dared to record

That the second shield I speak of,

Which was there for the rochets,

Was ever touched

But the English you should believe without doubt

All jousted with lance of steel

As long as their horses were able to run. [410]

There one was able to see well

The order of noble chivalry of France.

Many there took pleasure

When they came to couch the lances

One can see quite clearly

Which of them had renown,

Which party at the end

Had better done its desire

And the better shown its valor

Renaud de Roye, whom you know,

Was much prized in that field,

Those thirty days

By everyone.

Boucicaut was there exalted

And revered by many,

For he jousted most nobly

And Sempy did it grandly,

He struck many Englishmen hard.

Each of the three was feared by the English.

Whoever wished to render

A just judgement on the three

Should take care that he is well advised.

These are the three of whom I have spoken

For whom I have begun this poem.

For each has well deserved

That one should say of him

For very truth,

Much more than I am able.

Never such valor has been seen,

Many a day I was there,

Then I left, hale of body,

Joyful of heart

I went to Boulogne.

And made this truthful poem

I swear I have not been false,

Never have I added lies

It pleased God, noble king,

That, in this place, two or three days

You should have standing by you such friends

Who all were wise and courteous

And that you would have them

All three, joust against your enemies.

Well you should say that

The fleur de lis there had honor and worth

Through these three lords.

It is quite right that their deeds of arms are rewarded

And each of them is very well received

By all ranks and in all places.

All those who hear talk of it

I am sure,

Repent that they were not at that field.

Many ladies speak of it

When they hear about it

They wish good things

Concerning those who have jousted so well

Without being injured or wounded,

While wounding many in the joust

Great honor there they have gained.

Praise be to God in His majesty,

When they have come out of it so well

Now one is able fittingly to make

Many a good poem and many a song.

About the three lords named above

When they have come to the conclusion

Of their enterprise of renown,

Just as you have heard.

They are feared and dreaded

Everywhere they are honored

And there is a noble cause.

The English have much praised them for it

Because they have held themselves well,

Without pride or presumption.

After the jousts, by my faith,

It was beautiful to see the assembly

Of our people in the abbey

And how my lords, all three of them,

Went in noble array to fête the bachelors

They gave them supper with a cheerful countenance.

There was a noble company there

For a long time.

It was pleasant, with that music,

To see the happy festivities
And it could have been the court of the king.

There were many knights and squires
Doing the honors,
The fête was well prepared
Jean Piquet, Hostri de Bours
Maitres d'hôtel, for the thirty days
Were praised for the festivities
They gained great honor from it.

Now I will tell you, if you like
The names of the English who did the courses
In the fearful fête.
Two heralds of great renown,
Bourbon and Blue Greyhound
Have out of friendship
Given me the names.
I have not given the names in rhyme
Or in consonance at the least
One is not able to make a rhyme
In brief language without great displeasure
Often their names are too strong
To make a good rhyme.
…

In total, truly
One hundred and five jousted in all.
But I certainly do not wish to forget
That the noble earl of Derby
Had against each of our men
Five lances, right before my eyes.

I will not speak about the courses:

That belongs to the accounts

Of the noble men who were present

And to the heralds whom one saw there

Concerning Renaud de Roye, it is clear,

I can speak boldly

He pierced the arm of Blanquetin Hale,

Jousting is no joke!

And Christofle Lancheton

He struck, jousting with speed,

His lance into his face,

In front of all the nobility.

He sat through many other good blows

Of which you will hear.

The truth is, I do not know all of it.

But Boucicaut struck the lord of Beaumont all in a heap,

And threw his horse to the ground

Here my material says no more.

Another day, with a blow of his lance,

He bore down Lord Here Hansse

And Lord Here Hansse submitted,

So that the game came to an end.

And Sempy, the good knight,

Performed well in many cases,

For he bore the English Earl Marshal

To the ground along with his horse.

And in the last week

He bore down the captain of Niort

Whose name is [418]

Monseigneur Robert Electon,

With a very fine blow,

Without any blame
Just as the voices and praises
Of men of honor run after him.
To speak fittingly and rightly,
The French have had great honor from it.

Again you should know, my lord
That eight English have struck the shield
Who defaulted and did not joust.
That is the reason that each has heard these names:
Robert Gousel was
The first of the *malexcusés*;
Jehan de Haie, Jehan Strés,
Thomas Chele, to briefly say
Also Thomelin Ansetonne,
Failed to joust there.
Roger Langueferforte,
There did his duty very badly,
Regnault Bradesedebise
Did not fulfill his endeavor
Robert Seninlarde was not there at all.

I must tell you
That there were judges
Of this noble and grand celebration
The earl of Northumberland for the English
And for the French
A knight noble and courteous
Lancelot le Personne was his name.

Hear now the conclusion
Which I will tell you
So that you will know everything:

I saw the two shields taken down.

That of war the knight Lancelot took down,

And another more renowned

The lord of Saint-Saulieu, [419]

Took down then from its place

The shield for rochets.

Hostri de Bours was carrying

The lance. It was very fine to see the solemnities

There to see the trumpets of the king

And also see, in very noble array

Trumpets of the noble count de St. Pol.

I do not know how many

Singing noble minstrels took part.

And there the pursuivant of Sir Jehan de Roye

Was made a herald, a solemn joy,

And named "St. Inglevert" after the three knights,

And sworn in before the king of France.

Monk of St. Denis on St. Inglevert

While a truce endured and there was hope of peace between the French and the English, Englishmen of the highest nobility were able to cross to France freely for the sake of curiosity. There were always debates between the two groups concerning prowess and success in arms, and they argued about which of the two should be given more honor. The English were accustomed to keep silent about domestic calamities and to extoll their victories unendingly; which extremely displeased the French, who attributed that habit to presumption.

As a result those prominent knights and spirited youths, Renaud de Roye, Jean called le Maingre, alias Boucicaut, and the lord de Sempy, aflame with zeal and vigor, resolved to settle the matter through an unprecedented deed of arms, which is worthy of being recorded. So that they might restore the

worthy renown of the French chivalry and gain everlasting glory for the kingdom, they bound themselves by oath that they should measure their strength
against any foreign men at arms; and they begged permission from the king
with the strongest entreaties and obtained it with great difficulty, since in
the judgment of all prudent men, they were attempting a task beyond their
strength, since Sempy was puny and thin, Boucicaut of the same stature but
with better built limbs, and Renaud, likewise of medium size and superior to
the others only in nimbleness. Thus the prudent advised the comrades that
they should come to their senses and give up the project. They refused to do
so, responding over and over that "Nature doesn't deny small men constant
spirits." After gaining the king's support they had the deed of arms proclaimed
to all lords and ladies in neighboring countries and especially in England by
heralds accompanied by trumpeters. Without doubt this gave offense to the
ears of many critics and incited envious statements: "Now, without doubt, the
French are showing their pridefulness."

Near St. Inglevert, between Calais and Boulogne, lists were set up in a
level field, and there venerable men were stationed who courteously and with
friendly faces received arriving knights and squires and recorded the names
of those who wished to take part in the jousts. And so that all should be done
agreeably, and since the illustrious Frenchmen were inspired to undertake
the deed by love and by courage, they directed that worthy combat should
be offered in two forms, and to show this they had two shields hung in a
nearby hawthorn, so that when someone touched one of the shields it would
be clear what kind of combat he wished to undertake, and if he wished to
run five courses.

Knights and squires from England, Hainault, Lorraine and farther countries came forth, and scorned the shield of the hastilude as representing a
common and clownish exercise, touching the other which indicated war
with the point of their lances, swearing in this kind of fight to challenge the
Frenchmen to the utmost with all their might. It was enough to frighten
knights and veterans of worth, seeing the bodily beauty of the comers, which

was matched by their great strength. But as often as this, or the difficulty of the undertaking was mentioned to the Frenchmen, they always replied, "Prowess always loves to attempt hard and difficult things, and you know how young David killed the giant." This saying was considered with some justice to be presumptuous, and the project was constantly attributed to rashness and pride; and some prudent men rejected the plan, quite rightly as it appeared on the face of things. The way things worked out, though, a fortunate fate turned contempt into praise and glory.

Everything had been done so that the anticipated spectacle would win appropriate renown; the Frenchmen proceeded to tents decorated in royal fashion, in which banquets were to be celebrated for all foreign visitors over the course of thirty days. They spent three days greeting the first arrivals with due courtesy and then, on the twenty-first day of March, they met them in the lists in gleaming armor.

Then the following knights began the single combats: lord John Holland earl of Huntingdon, brother of the king of England, the Earl Marshal, the lords of Beaumont, of Clifford, Peter de Courtenay, John Galaffre, John Russell, Thomas de Sewinbourne; and these contended that day, with the fortune of battle going first one way then another.

[Following more enumerated jousts on the second day], four days were devoted to pleasant pastimes, so that they could give due honor to those who were arriving. Then they admitted to the next series of combats the following lords, namely John Holland, the Earl Marshal, [and nine more]. Their blows so bruised Boucicaut and Renaud that they had to keep to their beds for nine days, but thanks to the diligent care of the medical men whom the king had supplied them, along with other servants from the royal palace, they regained full health. During that time, however, lest the foreigners should become bored and leave, the Picard lord de Sempy, gathering up his strength and taking the turns of his comrades, powerfully withstood [15 jousters] and thus, by the judgment of the ladies, heralds and appointed judges he returned victorious to his comrades, to the sound of trumpets and singing.

FROISSART

Jean Froissart's Chronicles provides one of our finest accounts of the great jousts sponsored by the courts of France and England at the waning of the 14th century.

Froissart by Philippe Lemaire. Musée du Louvre, Paris, France.

The Monarch as the patron of knightly deeds of arms, and the arbiter of chivalric disputes: King Richard II sits on a throne under a red and gold canopy, surrounded by nobles, some in ermine capes, one in an ermine hat. A man in the foreground stoops, seemingly to pick up a glove that another man, left, has just thrown down as a challenge to a duel.

From Jean Froissart's *Chronicles*. Harl.4380.fol.141. British Library, London, Great Britain.

King Charles VI came to the throne a young, vigorous, charming monarch, much minded with chivalric deeds and displays of royal power—making his descent in madness all the more horrifying for France.

Royal 20 C. VII, Bibliotheque National, France.

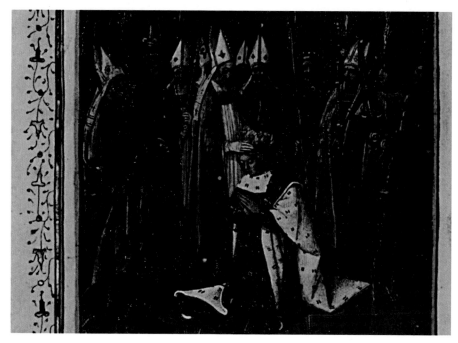

Detail of another image of the Coronation of Charles the VI, from the GRANDES CHRONIQUES DE FRANCE, by Jean Fouquet, created in the 15th century.

Coronation of Charles VI in 1380 in Reims, Jean Fouquet, 1460. Bibliotheque Nationale, Paris, France.

The entre of Queen Isabella into Paris, 1389, was the cause for célèbre. In this 15th-century depiction of the event, the Queen and her ladies, including the Duchess of Burgundy and Countess of Nevers, is greeted at the city gates by Charles VI.

From volume 4 of *The Chronicles* by Froissart. Harl 4380. British Library, London, Great Britain.

The accounts of the Jousts of St. Ingelvert are amongst our most detailed "blow-by-blow" records of the chivalric sport in the waning years of the 14th century.

From the *Chronicles* of Jean Froissart. (Bruges, 1470–1475). British Library, London, Great Britain.

The Smithfield Joust.

Illustration from *Chroniques*, by Jean Froissart, 14th c. Ms.5190, folio 88. Bibliotheque de l'Arsenal, Paris, France.

As the joust became a popular form of martial sport, a variety of safety measures when enacted to reduce catastrophes. The first of these, the barrier, prevented often fatal collisions between the riders.

Jousting between the Count Ferry de Lorraine and the Count d'Eu as the "Pas du Perron". *Recit du Tournoi de Roi Renee a Saumur en 1446.* Russian National Library, St. Petersburg, Russia

The joust as a social event: Renee d'Anjou, on the side of the defenders, prepares to fight the Duc d'Alencon. In a symbolic gesture, his lady leads his horse on a leash, in a direct homage to the Smithfield Jousts two generations earlier.

Recit du Tournoi de Roi Renee a Saumur en 1446 Nommee "Pas du Perron", 1470–1480. Russian National Library, St. Petersburg, Russia.

King Richard II presides over a tournament. 15th century, Flemish miniature.

Lambeth Palace Library, London, Great Britain.

By the 13th century a new form of knightly feat of arms, the joust, was beginning to rival the tournament in popularity. King Manfred of Sicily (c.1232–1266, r. 1258–1266), jousting with French knight in Sicily

Fresco, late 13th century, Tour Ferrande, Pernes-les-Fontaines, France

A tournament on the wall of the Knights' Hall in Runkelstein Castle, showing the relationship of the joust as a chivalric sport to court life and courtly entertainment. Below the jousting knights (left) a ballgame and (right) a roundelay, a medieval dance.

Fresco, Runkelstein Castle, 14th century.

Part of the joust's popularity with the chivalric class was its linking the knight to the great heroes of old, through its nature as a form of symbolic single combat.

Alexander, fighting Porus of India in single combat, charges and unhorses him with a thrust of his lance. Their respective armies look on. From *Le Livre et la vraye hystoire du bon roy Alixandre*. Roy 20 B XX. fol. 53. British Library, London, Great Britain.

Although eclipsed by the joust in popularity, the older, mounted tournament never fell entirely out of favor, and enjoyed a brief resurgence in the 15th century.

Worked wool tapestry, middle Rhine Region, c. 1410–1430. Museum of Applied Art, Frankfurt, Germany.

On the next day these Frenchmen honorably received the Bohemians, the Germans, and the English, and again powerfully fought [eight lords]. The day after was spent in enjoyment with all the noble lords and ladies, and after that they performed very dangerous combats with Henry earl of Derby, son of the duke of Lancaster, and with his retinue [of nine] and these were judged the most praiseworthy of all the foreigners.

In the absence of the lord de Sempy the other two comrades laudably completed the next contest [against ten opponents] …

In the last deed of arms, in which they met [eleven jousters], all those present judged that the French had performed mightily. But Robert de Rocheford was angry and hurried before the judges to complain that he had only fought four times with the lance, and refused to agree with the report given by the heralds. Boucicaut, seeing that obstinate spirit, and because he himself had done nothing more worthy than his companions had, boldly offered to make up the difference. Having gained the permission of the judges, Boucicaut rode against Rocheford so manfully that his lance pierced Rocheford's buckler and arm, and struck him and his horse to the ground. That unhappy man gained public infamy for perjury, and the deed of arms came to an end. The three Frenchmen had done so well that when the appointed judges were asked who had done the best, they praised them all equally and refused to make such comparisons.

Now that the time of jousting was finished, the Frenchmen treated their opponents with such generosity that they not only returned the arms and horses which they were entitled to on account of their victories, but, while saying their courteous farewells, loaded them with favors and very rich gifts.

Froissart on the Jousting at St. Inglevert

This deed of arms had been widely proclaimed, but especially in England, where it had caused much surprise, and excited several knights and squires, young adventurers and those who wished to perform deeds of arms, to confer on the subject. Some said they would be blameworthy, if they did not cross the sea, when the distance was so short to Calais, and pay a visit to these knights and try their skill at arms. … [U]pwards of one hundred knights and squires … said,—"Let us prepare ourselves to go to this place near Calais; for these French knights only hold it that they may have our company: it is well done, and shows they are good companions: let us not disappoint them!"

At the beginning of the charming month of May, the three before-mentioned young French knights were fully prepared to maintain their challenge at Saint Inglevert … On their arrival, they learnt that numbers of English knights and squires were come to Calais. They were overjoyed; and to hasten the business, and that news should be carried to the English, they ordered three rich vermilion-coloured pavilions to be pitched near the appointed place, and before each were suspended two targets, for peace or war, emblazoned with the arms of each lord. It was ordered that those who wished to ride and perform deeds of arms should touch, or send to have touched, one or both of these targets according to their pleasure, and they would be jousted with agreeably to their request.

On the 20th of May, as it had been proclaimed, the three knights were in their tents, properly armed and their horses ready saddled and equipped as the joust requires.

On the same day, those knights who were in Calais sallied forth, either as spectators or jousters, and on arrival drew up on one side. The place of the joust was smooth, green and grassy.

Sir John Holland [the earl of Huntingdon] was the first who sent his squire to touch the war-target of Sir Boucicaut, who instantly issued from his pavilion completely armed. He mounted his horse, and grasped his spear, which was stiff and well-steeled, and they took their distances. When the two knights had for a short time eyed each other, they spurred their horses and met full gallop with such force that Sir Boucicaut pierced the shield of the earl of Huntingdon, and the point of his lance slipped along his arm, but without wounding him. The two knights, having passed, continued their gallop to the end of the list and stopped in good order. This course was much praised. At the second course, they hit each other slightly, but no harm was done; and on the third lance their horses refused. The earl of Huntingdon, who wished to continue the joust, and was heated, returned to his place, expecting that Sir Boucicaut would take up his lance; but he did not, and showed by his expression and bearing that he would not joust with the earl any more that day.

Sir John Holland, seeing this, sent his squire to touch the war-target of the lord de Sempy. This knight, who had never refused a challenge, sallied out from his pavilion, and took his lance and shield. When the earl saw he was ready, he spurred his horse with a great will, as did the lord de Sempy. They couched their lances, and pointed them at each other. At the onset, their horses crossed; notwithstanding which, they met; but by this crossing, which was blamed, the earl was unhelmed. He returned to his people, who soon re-helmed him; and, having resumed their lances, they met full gallop, and hit each other with such force in the middle of their shields, that they would have been unhorsed had they not kept tight seats by the pressure of their legs against the horses' sides. They went to the proper places, where they refreshed themselves and took breath.

Sir John Holland, who had a great desire to perform his arms honorably, and grasped his spear again and braced himself; the lord de Sempy, seeing him advance, did not refuse him, but, spurring his horse on instantly, they gave blows on their helmets, that were luckily of well-tempered steel, which made sparks fly from them. At this course, the lord de Sempy lost his helmet; but the two knights briskly continued their career, and returned to their places.

This joust was much praised; and the English and French said, that the earl of Huntingdon, Sir Boucicaut, and the lord de Sempy, had jousted very well, without sparing or doing themselves any damage. The earl wished to break another lance in honor of his lady; but it was refused him. He then left the line, to make room for others, for he had run his six lances with such honor and grace as gained him praise from all sides.

A young and gallant knight of England was then ready, [Thomas Mowbray] the Earl Marshal, called the earl-marshal, who sent, according to the regulations, to touch the war-target of Sir Renaud de Roye. This being done, Sir Renaud came from his pavilion completely armed, and mounted his horse, which was ready for him: having had his shield and helmet buckled on, he seized his lance and took his distance. The two knights spurred their horses, but, at this first course, failed in their strokes, from their horses swerving out of the line, to their great vexation. Sir Renaud was hit with the second lance, and had his own broken. At the third course, they met with such force that sparks flew from their helmets, and the earl was unhelmed. He continued his career and returned quickly to his own place, but jousted no more that day, as he had done enough.

The Lord Clifford, a valiant knight, and cousin-german to the late Sir John Chandos, of great renown, then advanced, and sent to have the war-shield of Sir Boucicaut touched with a rod. Sir Boucicaut left his pavilion armed at all points and mounted his courser: he put his shield to his neck, was buckled up and put his lance in its rest. They met full gallop, and made the sparks fly from their helmets, but they neither broke their lances nor lost their stirrups: having passed, they returned to their places, eagerly preparing for the second course. They rode without sparing themselves: Sir Boucicaut broke his lance and was unhelmed, but did not fall to the ground. Lord Clifford returned to his place, to prepare himself for another course, but Sir Boucicaut did not again put on his helmet.

Lord Clifford, noticing this, resolved to perform arms with another knight, and sent his squire to touch the shield of the lord de Sempy. The lord de Sempy being ready, sallied forth from his pavilion; they ran at each other with great force, met full on, and Lord Clifford broke his lance into three pieces against the target of his adversary. In return, the lord de Sempy struck off his helmet, and both continued their career and returned to their places. The Lord Clifford jousted no more that day, for the spectators said he had conducted himself honorably and valorously.

Sir Henry Beaumont then came forward, and sent to have the target of Sir Boucicaut touched, who was instantly ready to reply to the call, having not dismounted from the jousts with Lord Clifford. The Lord Beaumont did not manage his lance well, and hit Boucicaut without effect; but Sir Boucicaut struck him so full on the middle of his shield that it drove him to the ground, and continued his course. Lord Beaumont was raised up by his attendants and remounted. The lord de Sempy then presented himself, and they jousted two courses very handsomely without hurt to either.

Sir Peter Courtenay, who was anxious to engage and to run six lances, sent a squire to touch with a rod the three shields of war. This caused a good deal of surprise, and he was asked what were his intentions by so doing. He replied that he wished to run against each of the French knights, if no misfortune befell him, and he entreated them to comply with his request. They agreed, and Sir Renaud de Roye first offered himself. Having made themselves ready, they spurred their horses with a great will, and took good aim not to miss their stroke; but, from the restiveness of their horses, they failed. They were much vexed, and returned to their places. On the second course, they met full gallop; and Sir Renaud de Roye, having unhelmed his adversary, returned gently towards his pavilion, his two courses being completed.

Sir Peter Courtenay being armed once more, the lord de Sempy advanced, and their lances were broken on their helms at the first shock: they continued their course, when new lances were given them. They advanced towards each other furiously, and the lord de Sempy hit Sir Peter without effect for his horse swerved a little; but Sir Peter struck off his helmet, and rode on at a gentle pace to his post.

Sir Boucicaut now came to complete the two other courses; and at their onset they struck each other on the shield so roughly that the two horses were suddenly checked in their career: no other damage ensued. At the second course, they were both unhelmed. When these six jousts were done, Sir Peter requested, as a favour, to run one more with any of the three knights who pleased, but it was refused; and he was told that he had done enough that day.

An English knight, called Sir John Gouloufre, came forth, armed at all points, and sent his squire to touch the war-shield of Sir Renaud de Roye, who was ready to joust; both advanced full gallop. They hit each other's helmets hard, but were neither unhelmed nor had their lances broken. Their horses refused to run the second course, to their great vexation. At the third joust they struck their shields and broke their lances. They were supplied with others, and, on their fourth course struck without effect. The fifth lance was too well employed, for they were both unhelmed, and then each rode to his own party.

Sir John Rousseau, an expert and valiant knight from England, but well known for his prowess in various countries, ordered his squire to touch the shield of the lord de Sempy, who was already armed and mounted. On receiving his lance, he spurred his horse against the English knight, and the shock of their spears against the targets instantly forced them to stop. Each returned to his post, and it was not long before they commenced their second course with equal vigour: but when near, the horses swerved, which prevented their stroke. To their sorrow, they were thus obliged to return again to the end of the lists. They were more successful the third course; for they struck each other with such force on the visors of their helmets that both were dishelmed: the knights continued their career, and the Englishman jousted no more that day.

Sir Thomas [*or* Peter] Shirborne, a young knight, but of good courage, sent his squire to touch the war-shield of Sir Boucicaut. The knight was ready to answer him, for he was armed and on horseback, his shield on his neck, leaning on his spear, to wait for an adventure. Perceiving himself called upon, he raised his spear, and looked to see what his adversary was doing, and observing that he was urging his horse forward, did the same. When they began their course, they couched their spears, thinking to make sure blows; but they were disappointed, to their great vexation, by the swerving of their horses, which forced them to return to their posts. They determined to manage them better at their second joust, and spurred them both so vigorously, they each struck the other on the visor. Sir Boucicaut broke his lance, but not so the English knight; for he employed it with such force, that he not only unhelmed, but made the blood spout from the nose of Sir Boucicaut as he broke off his helmet; Boucicaut then retired to his pavilion: he jousted no more that day, for it was now nearly vespers.

Sir Thomas Shirborne, however, would not desist until he had completed his number of lances: he, in consequence, sent his squire to touch the war-target of the lord de Sempy, who was prepared to meet him. The two knights spurred on violently against each other, and hit on the top of their helmets; but the lances slipped over, and they passed each other without hurt. The spectators said, had their spears been pointed lower, and the shields received the blows, one or both must have suffered severely or been borne to the ground. The next course, they struck full on their targets. The English knight's lance broke into three parts; but the blow of the lord de Sempy was so strong that the English knight lost his seat and fell to the ground, from whence, however, he instantly arose, and was led by his attendants from the lists.

The lord de Sempy returned to his post, viewing the state of the English adversary, and showing his willingness to renew the joust with him he had overthrown or with any other; but none came forward, as it was now time to leave off for this day, and return to their hôtels. The English, and such as had accompanied them, set off full gallop for Calais, where they remained that night enjoying themselves, and talking over the deeds of arms that had been performed. The French retired to Saint Inglevert; and, if the English talked much of what had been done, you may readily suppose the French were not silent.

On Tuesday, after mass and drinking a cup, all those who intended to joust, and those who wished to see them, left Calais, and rode in an orderly manner to where the lists had been held the preceding day. The French were already there, as was right, and prepared to receive them. The day was bright, clear, and sufficiently warm. The English drew up on one side, and armed those who were to joust.

...

Sir Nicholas Clifton, a young English knight, sent to touch the war target of the lord de Sempy, who immediately appeared ready armed and mounted. The two knights spurred their horses, bearing their spears in good array: when near, they lowered the spears and struck their opponent's target with such violence that the steel remained fixed; and it was a wonder that they were not badly injured, for they were both young, of good courage, and did not spare themselves. They neither fell nor were wounded, but their lances were shivered to pieces. They then passed on, each to his post. The second course was well jousted: they struck each on the helmets, but the blows did no damage, and they passed on. At the third course with lances, the horses crossed, to their sorrow, and they missed; and, at the fourth, the lord de Sempy unhelmed the English knight, who returned to his countrymen and did no more, for they assured him he had done enough and had acquitted himself valiantly, and that he must allow others to joust and perform their arms.

. . .

Sir Godfrey de Seca next presented himself: he was a gallant knight, and showed, by his manner of riding and bearing his lance, that he was an able jouster, and had a great desire to perform well. He sent his squire to touch the war-target of Sir Renaud de Roye. That knight came forward instantly, as he was ready mounted and arrayed, and he placed himself properly for the joust. They both set off at full gallop, and gave such blows on their targets that though their spears, from their strength, did not break, they bowed, and the combination of strong blows and strong arms stopped the horses in their tracks. Each knight returned to his post without losing his lance, but bore it handsomely before him. They went against each other again and met, but in crossing, which was the horses' fault, not the knights'. As they passed on they dropped their spears. Those nearby picked them up and returned them, and again they spurred their horses; for they were heated, and seemed unwilling to spare each other. The English knight hit Sir Renaud a very severe blow on the top of his helmet, without otherwise damaging him; but Sir Renaud gave him so strong a thrust on the target, (for at that time he was counted one of the stoutest jousters in France, and was so smitten with love for a young lady that it made all his affairs prosper) it pierced through it as well as his left arm: the spear broke as it entered, the butt end falling to the ground, the other sticking in the shield, and the steel in the arm. The knight, however, did not for this fail to finish his course gallantly; but his companions came to him, and the broken spear and steel were extracted, the blood stanched, and the arm tied up. Sir Renaud returned to his friends, and there remained, leaning on another lance that had been given him. Sir Renaud was much praised by the French and English for this joust; and no one said anything improper against him, because the Englishman had been wounded, for such are the events of arms: to one they are fortunate, to another the reverse; and, to say the truth, they did not spare each other.

...

Thomelin Messidon, a young English knight, well and richly armed, with a great desire to perform arms, sent to touch the shield of Sir Boucicaut. The knight instantly came forth, and, having grasped his lance, both spurred their horses; and each made his stroke by crossing under the helmet: they passed on without hurt or blame, but were not long before they spurred on again. In this course, they hit very roughly on the targets; Thomelin Messidon shivered his lance; but Sir Boucicaut's blow was so severe, it drove his opponent over the crupper of his horse to the ground. Those of his party ran to raise him up, and carried him off, for he jousted no more that day.

Another squire of England, called Waucreton, instantly stepped forth, and sent to touch the war-shield of Sir Boucicaut, saying he would revenge his companion, whom he had struck to the ground in his presence. Boucicaut was ready to answer him, being armed and mounted, and leaning on his spear. They met full gallop, and hit each other on the visors of their helmets, but passed on without other damage. Having had their helmets re-adjusted, and their lances given them, they again met with great violence, and from the shock of the blows on the targets, the horses were stopped, and the lances broken into three pieces, but they completed their course without any hurt. They had new spears given them; and at the third course Sir Boucicaut was hit hard on the target, but he gave Waucreton a blow that unhelmed him: he then withdrew to his countrymen, and jousted no more that day; for they said he had done enough, and acquitted himself well.

...

You must know, though I have not before made mention of it, that King Charles of France was present at these jousts. Being young, and desiring to witness extraordinary sights, he would have been much vexed if he had not seen the jousts. He was therefore present from the beginning to end, attended only by the lord de Garencieres; but both were so disguised that nobody knew of it; and they returned every evening to Marquise.

The ensuing day, Wednesday, was as fine as the foregoing; and the English, who had crossed the sea to take part in or view these French deeds, mounted their horses, at the same hour as on the preceding day, and rode to the place appointed for the lists, to the delight of the French, who were rejoiced to see them. It was not long after their arrival when an English squire, a good jouster called John Savage, squire of honor and of the body to the earl of Huntingdon, sent to touch the shield of war of Sir Renaud de Roye. The knight answered, he was ready and willing to satisfy him. When he had mounted his horse, and had his shield buckled and lance given to him, they set off full gallop, and gave such blows, on the targets, that had the spears not broken, one or both must have fallen to the ground. This course was handsome and dangerous; but the knights received no hurt, though the points of the lances passed through the targets, and slipped off the side. The spears were broken about a foot from the shaft, the points remaining in the shields; and they gallantly bore the shafts before them, as they finished their career. The spectators thought they must have been seriously wounded; and the French and English hastened each to their companion, whom, to their joy, they found unhurt.

They were told they had done enough for that day but John Savage was not satisfied, and said he had not crossed the sea to run one lance. This was reported to Sir Renaud, who replied,—"He is in the right; and it is right just that he should be gratified in all respects, either by me or by one of my companions." When they had rested themselves a while, and received new shields and lances, they began their second course, each aiming well at the other; but they missed because their horses crossed, to their great vexation, and returned to their posts. Their lances, which they had thrown to the ground in anger, were given to them, and they set off on their third course. This time they hit on the visors of their helmets; and the points became attached in such a way that both were unhelmed as they passed. The joust was much applauded for its correctness and vigour. When they were returned to their posts, the English told John Savage that he had done enough and that he should honorably withdraw, and must allow others to joust as well as himself. He complied with this, and, laying aside his lance and target, dismounted, and sat on a hackney to see the others ride.

…

… a young and frisky English knight advanced, who was eager to conquer honor. His name was Sir John Clifton, and he bore for arms a field argent, fretted azure, and on a chief azure a mullet argent. The knight was equipped at all points as the feats required, and he sent his squire to touch the war-shield of Sir Renaud de Roye. This knight responded, for he was ready and very pleased by the approach of the other.

Each took his position on his own side. They were given their lances and took them and put them in the rests, and then they spurred the horses with great force. On this first course they struck each other on the helms and went on and finished their runs and then returned to their sides. They still kept their lances in their rests. They scarcely paused before they spurred their horses and came against each other, struck each others' shields, and gave great blows; but they did not harm each other. The lances fell to the ground, but people were ready to pick them up. The two knights returned to their sides very briskly. They were given their lances; they spurred their horses and struck each other. On this third blow they struck high on the helmets so hard that the raised sparks, then passed on. On the fourth lances their horses crossed, which greatly angered them. The fifth course was well-ridden, for each broke his lance.

The two knights were inflamed against each other, and plainly showed that they had a great desire to joust and prove themselves. When they had come back to their own sides, they were given good and strong lances. They hardly paused before they spurred their horses with great force, and came against each other. On this sixth lance they struck each other so that both were unhelmed. This joust was highly praised by all who saw it. The knights passed on and finished their turns, and then each returned to his own people. The English knight jousted no more that day, for he had done enough.

...

The English now collected together, as evening was approaching, and returned to Calais, where they passed the night in talking over the different deeds
of arms that had been that day performed. The French amused themselves in
like manner at Saint Inglevert.

On Thursday morning, the fourth day of the week, the English found that
there were yet many knights and squires who had not entered the lists, and
who had purposely come from England; they therefore said, that all who
had any intentions to joust should do so, otherwise they would not be handsomely treated. The lords of England had agreed to return to Saint Inglevert
on the Thursday, and let those who wished to perform their arms do so. In
consequence, they left Calais after mass, and, on arriving at the lists, found
the three French knights ready in their pavilions to answer all who might
call on them, attended by those that were to serve them and such as came to
witness the deeds of arms.

...

A Bohemian knight now advanced, who was of the household of the queen of
England, called Sir Here-Hance. He was considered a strong and good jouster,
and bore for his arms argent, three griffins' feet sable, ongled azure. When he
came to the line, he was asked which of the three knights he wished to joust
with: he replied, "With Boucicaut."

On this, an English squire was sent, according to the regulations, to touch Sir
Boucicaut's war-target. The knight was ready and mounted on his courser. His
shield was buckled on, and he took his lance and put it in its rest, and looked
over the knight who was also ready to joust, with his shield at his neck and his
lance in his fist. They spurred their horses with a great will, and came together,
thinking to give full strokes; but that did not happen, for the Bohemian knight
committed a fault, for which he was greatly blamed. He had, out of the line of
jousting, hit Sir Boucicaut on the helmet and continued his career. The English
saw that he indeed was at fault, and would forfeit his arms and horse, should
the French insist upon them. The French and English held a long conversation

on this ill-placed stroke; but at last the three French knights pardoned him, the better to please the English.

Here-Hance begged as a favour that he might be permitted to run only one course more. When he was asked which of the three he wished, he sent to touch the target of Sir Renaud de Roye. That knight was waiting in his pavilion, not having jousted that day, but came forward all ready and declared his willingness to accommodate Sir Here-Hance, since his request had been granted. Sir Renaud mounted his horse. His shield was buckled on. He was given his lance. He took it and put it in the rest, put all his will into reaching and striking the Bohemian. Both spurred their horses at the same moment, lowered their lances as they approached, and hit in the shields. Sir Renaud (who was one of the strongest and toughest jousters in France) thrust with such force that the Bohemian flew completely out of his saddle, and fell so severely on the ground that the spectators imagined he was killed. The other knight passed on and made his turn, and returned to his post. Here-Hance was raised with much difficulty by his attendants, and carried back among them. The English were happy that he had been struck down, for the uncourteous manner in which he had run his first course, and I tell you that he had not any desire to joust more that day.

An English squire called Nicholas Lamb, well and elegantly armed, advanced, having a great desire to try his skill in arms. He sent to strike the war-target of the lord de Sempy, who was already mounted and armed, with his buckler on his breast, blazoned with his arms. He grasped his spear, and flew to the lists with the eagerness of a hawk to seize his prey. The English squire did the same, and, setting off at full speed, they gave such blows on their bucklers, that their lances were shivered: it was fortunate they broke, or the knights must have been greatly hurt, or unhorsed, but they kept their seats firmly. When returned to their stations, they were supplied with new lances and with them, at the second course, made sparks fly from their helmets: no other damage was done, for the spears had crossed, and they continued their career to their posts. After a short rest, they commenced their third joust, and had well examined where they could best place their thrusts. This was gallantly performed; for they hit, justly, the visors of the helmets, and the points of the lances entered and stuck: both were so neatly unhelmed, that the lacings burst, and the helmets flew over the cruppers of their horses and onto the field. The knights kept their seats and completed their course in handsome array, and then returned to their countrymen.

The jousting then came to an end, for no more Englishmen came forward. All those knights who had jousted the preceding days went in a body before the French knights, and thanked them warmly for the amusements they had given them. They said,—"All the knights and squires of our company who wanted to joust with you have done so. So we take our leave of you, and return to Calais on our way to England. We know well that whoever may wish to joust with you and try their skill in arms will find you here for thirty days according to your proclamation. We assure you that on our return to England, we shall tell all knights and squires what we have seen, and tell and entreat them to come and see you."

"Many thanks," replied the three knights: "they shall be made welcome, and delivered according to the law of arms as you have been; and we desire you will accept our best acknowledgments for the courtesy you have shown us."

In this friendly manner the English and French knights separated, in the plain of St. Inglevert: the first took the road to Calais, but made no long stay; ... The three French knights before named kept their engagements valiantly at St. Inglevert.

From the time the Englishmen I have spoken of left Calais, I never heard that any others came from England to St. Inglevert to try their skill in arms. ... The three knights, however, remained there until the thirty days were fully accomplished and more, and then leisurely returned each to his home. When they waited on the king of France, the duke of Touraine and other lords at Paris, they were most handsomely received. Indeed, they were entitled to such reception, for they had gallantly behaved themselves, and upheld the honor of the king and of the realm of France.

Book of the Deeds of Boucicaut on St. Inglevert (Anonymous)

You should know that Sir Boucicaut had been in his youth commonly on journeys with the good duke of Bourbon, who for the good will that he had seen in him right from his first beginnings, had kept him in his household and with him, as has been said before. It happened that when the king was at Cluny, as it was said, that because of the great good which he saw increasing every day in Boucicaut, he loved him more than any, as much as if the love had begun in early childhood. So he wished to have him always in his company and in fact asked for him from the duke of Bourbon, who was content for the advancement of Boucicaut, and thus he became completely one of the court of the king, and he went with him in that journey to Languedoc.

As Love and chivalric Valor often counsel the hearts of the good to venture honorable things to increase their worth and their honor, during this journey it happened that Boucicaut planned a very high undertaking, the most gracious and honorable which a knight had ventured in Christendom for a long time. And it should be noticed and seen in the deeds of this valiant man, how without doubt just as the proverb says, that it is by works, and not at all by words, that the spirits of valiant, gallant men show themselves, for there is no doubt that the man who has the spirit and desire to reach and attain honor never thinks but to consider how and in what way he ought to do such deeds, that he should deserve being called valiant; nor ever should it seem to him that he has done enough, whatever good thing he should do, to acquire praise for his valour and prowess. And that this is true, we see demonstrated by the works of this valiant knight Boucicaut; because of the great desire which he had to be valiant and to acquire honor, he had no other care except to think how he could spend his beautiful youth in chivalrous pursuits. And because it appeared to him that he was not able to do enough, he took no rest; for immediately that he had achieved some good deed he attempted another. Such was the endeavor which, after which he had been given leave by the king, he had proclaimed in many realms and Christian countries, namely in England, Spain, Aragon, Germany, Italy and others. He made it known to all princes, knights and squires that he, accompanied by two knights, one named Sir Renaud de Roye, the other the lord de Sempy, would hold the field of combat for the space of thirty days, without leaving, if no reasonable excuse should come to them, namely from the twentieth day of April, at the place called St. Inglevert, between Calais and Boulogne. There would the three knights await all comers, ready and equipped to joust with all knights and squires who required it of them, without missing a day excepting Fridays; and it should be known that each one of the said knights would give five strokes of a steel lance or a rochet to all those who should be enemies of the realm, who required the strokes from one of them, and who would give to each one having any other need such good care that everything, before the thirty days began, should be so well and so beautifully prepared that nothing should be lacking.

When the first day of the said undertaking had come, the three knights were all armed and ready in their pavilions awaiting whoever might come. Sir Boucicaut was especially richly equipped. And because he thought it a good thing—since before the end of the game an abundance of foreigners, Englishmen and others would come there—that each should see that he was ready and equipped, if anyone required anything from him, to release them and do such deeds of arms as anyone wished to ask of him, for this reason he took then the motto that he never after let go of, which is this: "Whatever you wish." He had it put on all his badges, and there he carried it for the first time.

The English who always had had animosity toward the French and who willingly took pains at all times to do them harm and surpass them in all things, if they were able, had well heard and understood the announcement of this above said honorable undertaking. So most of them, and the higher ranking among them said that the game should certainly not take place without them. So they did not forget, as soon as the first day of the undertaking was come, to be there in a good company of the greatest men of England, as one may presently hear in detail.

On the first day, as Sir Boucicaut was waiting all armed in his pavilion, and also his companions in theirs, there came Sir John Holland, brother of King Richard of England, who, with a very fine company, all armed on his destrier, the minstrels sounding horns before, took himself onto the field. And there he stood, in a very exalted manner, and in the presence of a great abundance of noble men who attending, went all over the field; and then, when he had done this, he went from corner to corner in a very exalted manner, and afterwards one laced his bascinet on him, which was strongly buckled. Then he went to strike Boucicaut's shield of war, which choice he had well considered. After this blow, the noble knight Boucicaut did not delay at all; holding himself straighter than a rush, on his good destrier, the lance at his neck, minstrels before him, and well attended by some of his people, you should have seen how he leaped from his pavilion and went and placed himself at the line; and there he stopped a little, then lowered his lance and put it in rest, and spurred towards his adversary who was a very valiant knight and who also spurred back towards him. They did not fail to meet, so that they gave each other very great blows on the shields which made both their backs bend, and their lances fly into pieces. The crowd loudly cried out their names; so they took their turn, and new lances were given to them, and once again they ran against each other and likewise they struck against each other. And thus they completed their five strokes seated, all with steel lances, both of them so valiantly that neither of them ought to have reproach. It should be noted that at the fourth blow, after the lances were broken in pieces, because of the great fervor of the good destriers who were running strongly, the two knights crashed into each other in such a collision that the horse of the Englishman fell to the earth on its hindquarters and would have fallen over without fail if the strength of the man had not held him up. Boucicaut's horse wavered but did not fall at all.

After this joust and the number of blows was achieved, the two knights went back in the pavilions; but Boucicaut was not allowed to rest there for very long, for there were many other valiant English knights who, like the first, required him to joust with the lance of steel. In that same day he delivered two others and performed his fifteen seated blows so well and so valiantly that of all he acquitted himself with very great honor. While Boucicaut jousted, just as has been said, do not think that his companions were at all idle, for they had found that they had attracted many to joust with them, and all with steel lances. So they both did so well and so fine that the honors went to their side.

I do not know why I should prolong my account by describing the details of all the blows delivered by each of them, which would bore my listeners; but keep things brief, I tell you that the principal ones who jousted with Boucicaut while the thirty days lasted were, first the one of whom we have already spoken, and then the earl of Derby who you will hear claims to be Henry, king of England (who jousted with him ten strokes with a steel lance, for when he had jousted the five strokes according to the proclamation, the duke of Lancaster, his father, wrote to Boucicaut that he had sent his son to him to learn from him, for he knew him to be a very valiant knight, and he entreated him that he should agree to joust ten strokes with him), the Earl Marshal, the lord of Beaumont, Sir Thomas de Percy, the lord of Clifford, the lord of Courtenay, such knights and squires of the said realm of England to the number of twenty-six, and of other countries, such as Spaniards, Germans and others, more than forty. And they all jousted with the steel lance. And to all Boucicaut and his companions provided the number of blows, except some who were not able to achieve them because they were wounded; for many of the English were borne to the ground, riders and horses, and were badly wounded by the stroke of the lance. And the same Sir John Holland spoken of above was so badly wounded by Boucicaut that he was not far from death, and similarly some other foreigners; but the valiant and noble Boucicaut and his good and proven companions, thanks to God, suffered no harm or wound. And thus the good knights continued their noble undertaking each day until the term of thirty days was accomplished. And thus he leaped up to very great honor in the eyes of the king and chivalry of France, and he received such great praise for him and his companions that it always will be spoken of. So Boucicaut left there with his people, and returned to Paris where he was very joyously received by the king and all the lords and he was also fêted and honored by some ladies, for he deserved it.

5.

The Joust at Smithfield near London, October 1390

The Cry (Announcement)

Translation by Will McLean

Hear ye, lords, knights, and squires. We make known to you a very great deed of arms and very noble Joust that will be performed by a knight, who will carry a red shield, with on it a white hart having a crown around its neck with a hanging chain of gold, on a green bank. And the said knight accompanied by twenty knights all dressed in one color. And then to come Sunday, the ninth day of October next into the new Abbey near the Tower of London.

And from that place these same knights will be led by twenty ladies dressed in one livery, of the same color and suite as the said knights, all around the outside of the noble city called New Troy, otherwise known as London. And just outside the same gate the said knights will hold the field called Smithfield by the Hostel of Saint John called Clerkwell. And there they will dance, and sing and lead a joyous life.

And the following Monday the said twenty knights, in one livery as afore-said, will be within the said field of Smithfield, armed and mounted within the lists, before the hour of High Prime, to deliver all manner of knights who wish to come and joust, each one of them of six lances, such as they will find within the tourney field, the which lances will be carried according to the standard. The standard will be in the same field, and by that standard all the lances will be measured so that they are the same length. And the said twenty knights will joust in high saddles. And all the lances will be fitted with ap-propriate coronels. And the shields of the said knights will be covered neither with iron nor steel.

At those jousts the noble ladies and damsels will give the knight who jousts best of those without a horn garnished with gold, and they will give to the one who jousts best of those within a white greyhound with a collar of gold around its neck. And the following Wednesday the same twenty knights aforesaid will come to the said field to deliver all knights and squires whatever with as many lances as it pleases them to joust with. And the noble ladies will give a circlet of gold to the one who jousts best of those without. And the one within that jousts best will be given a golden belt. And the lady or damsel who dances best or leads the most joyful life those three days aforesaid, that is to say Sunday, Monday, and Tuesday, will be given a golden brooch by the knights. And the lady who dances and revels best after her, which is to say the second prize for those three days, will be given a ring of gold with a diamond.

And whoever jousts the said three days with a lance that is not according to the measure of the standard will neither carry away nor be given any manner of prize or degree. And whoever jousts with a lance without an appropriate coronel will lose their horse and their harness.

And the Wednesday following the said three days of the said jousts, sixteen squires carrying red shields, and on those shields a silver griffon, mounted, armed, and riding in high saddles with white sockets and shields as aforesaid, will hold the field and deliver all knights and squires who come of as many lances as seem good to them.

And there will be given in the same field to whoever jousts best of those without a noble courser, saddled and bridled. And whoever jousts best of those within will be given a fine chaplet well worked with silk.

And by virtue of the noble pardon of arms, surety will be given to all foreign knights and squires who wish to come to the said festival. And to remain and spend twenty days before the festival and twenty days afterward, by virtue of the truce given and agreed by the two kings without any hindrance being given to them. And concerning that matter, all who wish will have safe conduct from the king our sovereign lord.

Froissart's Account of the Joust

News of the splendid feasts and entertainments made for Queen Isabella's public entry into Paris was carried to many countries, and very justly, for they were most honorably conducted. The king of England and his three uncles had received the fullest information of them: for some of his knights had been present, who had reported all that had passed with the utmost fidelity. In imitation of this, the king of England ordered grand celebrations to be held in the city of London, where sixty knights should be accompanied by sixty noble ladies, richly ornamented and dressed.

The sixty knights were to joust for two days; that is to say, on the Sunday after Michaelmas-day, and the Monday following in the year of grace 1390. The sixty knights were to set out at two o'clock in the afternoon from the Tower of London, with their ladies, and parade through the streets, down Cheapside, to a large square called Smithfield. There the knights were to wait on the Sunday the arrival of any foreign knights who might be desirous of jousting; and this festivity on the Sunday was called the celebration of the challenge.

The same ceremonies were to take place on the Monday, and the sixty knights to be prepared for jousting courteously with blunted lances against all corners. The prize for the best knight of those without was to be a rich crown, of gold, that for those within of the lists a very rich golden clasp: they were to be given to the most gallant jouster, according to the judgment of the ladies, who would be present with the Queen of England and the great barons as spectators.

On the Tuesday, there would be at the same place sixty squires well-mounted and armed for the joust, and all squires, foreign and English, who wished to come and joust would do so. And they would be courteously received with blunted lance. The prize for those without was a courser saddled and bridled, and for those within the lists a very fine falcon.

The manner of holding this feast being settled, heralds were sent to proclaim it throughout England, Scotland, Hainault, Germany, Flanders, and France. It was ordered by the council to what parts each herald was to go; and, having time beforehand, they published it in most countries.

Many knights and squires from foreign lands made preparations to attend it: some to see the manners of the English, others to take part in the tournaments. On the feast being made known in Hainault, Sir William de Hainault count d'Ostrevant, who was at that time young and gallant, and fond of jousting, determined, in his own mind, to be present and to honor and make acquaintance with his cousin, King Richard, and his uncles whom he had never seen. He therefore engaged many knights and squires to accompany him; in particular the lord de Gomegines, because he was well known in England, having lived there some time. Sir William resolved, while his preparations were making, to visit his father, the count of Hainault, Holland, and Zealand, to speak with him on the subject, and to take leave of him before he went to England. ...

During this visit, he told his father his intentions to partake of the great feast in England, to see his cousins and other English lords whom he was desirous of knowing.

"William," replied the count, "my good son, you have nothing to do in England: you are now connected by marriage with the blood royal of France, and your sister is the wife of the eldest son of our cousin the duke of Burgundy: you have no occasion, therefore, to seek other connections."

"My lord," answered Sir William, "I do not wish to go to England to form any alliance, but merely to joust and enjoy this feast, which has been publicly proclaimed everywhere, and visit my cousins, whom I have never seen. Should I not go thither, after the particular invitation I have had, for a purpose messenger brought it to me, my refusal will be considered as the effect of pride and presumption. I feel myself bound therefore in honor to go, and I beg, father, that you will not refuse me your consent."

"William," replied the count, "you are your own master; act as you please; but I should think, for the sake of peace, it were better you did not go."

The count d'Ostrevant, perceiving this subject was disagreeable to his father, turned the conversation to other matters; but his resolution was fixed … His herald, Gomegines, was sent to England to inform the king and his uncles, that he would come honorably attended to his feast. They were much pleased at this intelligence, and presented the herald with great gifts, which were very acceptable, for he became blind towards the end of his days. I know not if he had angered God, that he was afflicted with such a punishment; but this herald, when in power, had behaved, with so much insolence, that he was little pitied in his distress.

…

The count d'Ostrevant set out from Hainault with a numerous attendance of knights and squires, and travelled through Artois to St. Omer and then to Calais, where he met the count de St. Pol. When the wind was favourable, and their attendants embarked, they crossed the channel; but it was told me, and I believe it, that the count de St. Pol arrived in England three days before the count d'Ostrevant and then came to London, where he found the king and his brother-in-law, Sir John Holland, who with many other nobles, received him with great joy, and enquired about the news from France, and he answered cogently and wisely. The count d'Ostrevant having crossed the sea, stopped at Canterbury, and on the Friday morning, without breaking his fast, paid his devotions at the shrine of Thomas à Becket, making at the same time a very rich offering at that altar. He remained that whole day at Canterbury, and on the following went to Rochester. On account of his numerous train, he travelled but a short day's journey, to spare his horses that carried the baggage. Sunday after mass he left Rochester and dined at Dartford, whence he continued his journey to London, for it was on this Sunday that the festivities were to begin.

This Sunday, according to proclamation, being the next to Michaelmas day, was the beginning of the festivities at Smithfield, which was called the challenge ... About three o'clock, there paraded out from the Tower of London, which is situated in the square of St. Catherine, on the banks of the Thames, sixty barded coursers prepared for the joust, on each was mounted a squire of honor that advanced only at a foot's pace; then came sixty ladies of rank, mounted on palfreys most elegantly and richly dressed, following each other, every one leading a knight with a silver chain completely armed and prepared for jousting; and in this procession they moved on through the streets of London, attended by numbers of minstrels and trumpets, to Smithfield. The queen of England and her ladies and damsels were already arrived and placed in chambers handsomely decorated. The king was with the queen. When the ladies who led the knights arrived in the square, their servants were ready to assist them to dismount from their palfreys, and to conduct them to the apartments prepared for them. The jousters remained until their squires of honor had dismounted and brought them their coursers, which having mounted, they had their helmets laced on, and prepared themselves in all points for the joust.

The count de Saint Pol with his companions now advanced, handsomely armed in harness of war for the occasion, and the festivities began. Every foreign knight who pleased jousted, or had time and space for so doing, before the evening set in. The jousting challenge was well done and continued until night fell. The lords and ladies then retired where they had made appointments. The queen was lodged in the bishop of London's palace near St. Paul's church, where the banquet was held.

Towards evening, the count d'Ostrevant arrived, and was kindly received by King Richard and his lords. The prize for those without was adjudged to the Count Waleran de St. Pol, and that for those within to the earl of Huntingdon. The dancing took place at the queen's residence, in the presence of the king, his brothers, his uncles and the barons of England. The ladies and damsels continued their amusements, before and after supper, until it was time to retire, when all went to their lodgings, except the king and the queen, who then were staying at the palace of the bishop.

You would have seen on the ensuing morning, Monday, squires and valets busily employed, in different parts of London, furbishing and making ready armor and horses for their masters who were to engage in the jousts. In the afternoon, the king of England entered Smithfield armed and magnificently accompanied by dukes, counts and lords, for he was chief of those within of the lists. The queen went to the place where the jousts were held with her ladies, in the apartments that had been prepared for them. The count d'Ostrevant came next, with a large company of knights and squires from his country, fully armed for jousting; then the count de Saint Pol and the knights from France, who had a great will to joust.

The jousts now began, grand and beautiful jousts, and they were well done, and every one exerted himself to the utmost to excel: many were unhorsed, and many lost their helmets. And these strong and fierce jousts continued until night, when they all retired to their hôtels … There was a great and well-prepared supper. And that day's prize for those without was adjudged, by the ladies, lords, and heralds, to the count d'Ostrevant, who far eclipsed all who had jousted that day; that for those within was given to a gallant knight of England called Sir Hugh Spenser.

On the morrow, Tuesday, the jousts were renewed by the squires, who jousted in the presence of the king and queen, until night, when all retired as on the preceding day. The supper was as magnificent as before at the palace of the bishop, where the king, queen and ladies lodged; and the dancing lasted until day-break, when the company broke up. On Wednesday after dinner all the knights and squires who were inclined to joust did so all together. And the jousts were strong and fierce and well-performed; they lasted until night, and the supper for the ladies was as the preceding day.

On Thursday, the king entertained at supper all the foreign knights and squires, and the queen their ladies and damsels. The duke of Lancaster gave a grand dinner to them on the Friday. On Saturday, the king and the lords left London for Windsor, whither the count d'Ostrevant, the count de St. Pol, and the foreign knights who had been present at the feasts, were invited. All accepted the invitation, as was right, and went to Windsor, which has a handsome castle, well built and richly ornamented, situated on the Thames twenty miles from London. The entertainments were very magnificent in the dinners and suppers King Richard made, for he thought he could not pay honor enough to his cousin the count d'Ostrevant. He was solicited by the king and his uncles to be one of the companions of the Order of the Blue Garter, as the chapel of St. George, the Order's patron, was at Windsor. In answer to their request, he said he would consider of it, and instantly consulted the lord de Gomegines and the bastard Fierabras de Vertain, who were far from discouraging him from accepting the order. He returned to the king, and was admitted a knight companion of the Garter, to the great surprise of the French knights then present. …

Thus was the count d'Ostrevant blamed by the French, without the smallest cause; for what he had done was no way to injure the crown of France, nor his cousins and friends of that country. Nothing was farther from his mind than any hostility to the king of France; but he had accepted the Garter to oblige his cousins in England, and on occasion to be a mediator between the two countries. When he took the oaths usual on the admission of knights to the Order, it ought to be known publicly that nothing was said or done prejudicial to France, nor any treaties entered into with that intent. I mention this, since it is impossible to prevent the envious from spreading abroad their tales. …

Rumour, which magnifies everything, carried to the king of France, his brother, and uncles, every particular that had passed at this feast in England. Those who had been there confirmed it, nothing was forgotten, but rather additions made with the intent of doing mischief in preference to good … The king of France and his uncles, on hearing this, were much troubled and vexed with the count d'Ostrevant. … The duke of Burgundy, whose daughter the count had married, was highly displeased at these reports; for he had always pushed his son-in-law as much as he could into the good graces of the king and the royal family. This business was not neglected; for the king of France wrote very sharp letters to the count d'Ostrevant, which he sent to him at Quesnoy, commanding him to come to Paris, and, in the presence of the peers of France, do homage for the county of Ostrevant, or he would make war upon him, and dispossess him of it. …

The detail of all that passed would be too long for such a history as this, that embraces so many objects. The conclusion was, that notwithstanding the support of the duke of Burgundy, the count d'Ostrevant was forced to go to Paris to perform his duty, and acknowledge his holding the county of Ostrevant from the crown of France, otherwise he would have had war instantly carried into Hainault. The lord de Coucy and Sir Oliver de Clisson took much pains that a war should ensue; but the lord de la Riviere and Sir John le Mercier counteracted them to the utmost of their power.

Appendix

Summarizing Froissart's Account of the St. Inglevert Jousting

In the following table I show the records of the three French champions during the four days of jousting described by Froissart.

We cannot be certain how various results of a joust were evaluated at this time. There is no hint of the kind of point-counting that was done in the fifteenth century and later. Froissart seems to show that qualitative judgment of a competitor's handling of horse and lance was more important than an abstract count; in fact, both riders were sometimes considered to have done equally well.

In the 1350s, unhorsing one's opponent (according to Geoffroi de Charny's *Questions*) resulted in the opponent forfeiting his mount; only the Monk of St. Denis mentions forfeiture of horses (and arms) in connection with St. Inglevert, but he says that the three Frenchmen waived their rights to such prizes.

Froissart recorded the result of 137 courses run by the French champions. Whether his description reflects reality is hard to know, as I have noted above. We can perhaps only say that Froissart shows us what a joust of the highest quality should have looked like to appreciative connoisseurs. For most of us modern readers, the story is a bit repetitive. I hope that this simplified presentation will make it easier to come to grips with.

	Boucicaut	Roye	Sempi	Totals
Opponents	18	12	16	46 (39)*
Courses	50	41	46	137
Lost helm	7	4	9	20
Unhelmed opponent	12	7	12	31
Broke lance on opponent	5	5	6	16
Had lance broken on him	5	4	8	17
Unhorsed opponent	3	2	3	8

* Adding the number of English and allied opponents each French knight faced yields 46; but the French in fact faced only 39 distinct persons.

In 18 of the 137 courses, the horses swerved or refused to the point that the combatants did not strike each other at all.

I have not counted such occurrences as lances being dropped, shields being pierced, or horses being stopped in mid-career.

Bibliography

Texts and Translations

Chronographia Regum Francorum, ed. H. Moranville. 3 vols. Paris, 1891–7.

Chronique du Religieux de Saint-Denys, ed. M. Bellaguet. 6 vols. Paris, 1839–52.

Cripps-Day, Francis Henry. *The Tournament in England and France.* London: Bernard Quaritch, 1918. Appendix V contains the Cry of the Smithfield joust.

Deschamps, Eustache. *Œuvres complètes de Eustache Deschamps,* ed. Queux de Saint-Hilaire. 11 vols. Societe des anciens textes français. Paris, 1878–1903.

Froissart, Jean. *Chronicles,* trans. Thomas Johnes. 2 vols. London, 1862.

———. *Œuvres,* ed. Kervyn de Lettenhove. 25 vols. Brussels, 1867–77.

Joustes de Saint-Inglebert, 1389–1390. Poème contemporaine, ed. J. Pichon in *Partie inédite des chroniques de Saint-Denis.* Paris, 1864. Pp. 59–78.

Le Livre de fais du bon messire Jehan le Maingre, dit Boucicaut, Mareschal de France et Gouverneur de Jennes, ed. Denis Lalande. Geneva : Droz, 1985.

Secondary works

Barber, Richard and Juliet Barker, *Tournaments: Jousts, chivalry and pageants in the Middle Ages.* Woodbridge: Boydell Press, 1989.

Barker, Juliet. *The Tournament in England 1100–1400.* Woodbridge: Boydell Press, 1986.

Gaucher, Elisabeth. "Les joutes de Saint-Inglevert: Perception et écriture d'un évenement historique pendant la guerre de Cent Ans," *Le Moyen Âge* 102 (1996): 229–43.

Kipling, Gordon. *Enter the King: Theatre, liturgy and ritual in the medieval civic triumph.* Oxford: Clarendon Press, 1998.

Muhlberger, Steven. *Deeds of Arms: Formal combats in the late fourteenth century.* Highland Village, TX: Chivalry Bookshelf, 2005.

———. *Jousts and Tournaments: Charny and chivalric sport in fourteenth-century France.* Union City: Chivalry Bookshelf, 2003.

Palmer, J.J.N. *England, France and Christendom 1377–99.* London: Routledge and Kegan Paul, 1972.